Standing Liberty Quarters

Third Edition

By
J.H. Cline

For further information contact:
J. H. Cline
33920 U.S. 19-N. #230
Palm Harbor, Florida 34684
or
P.O. Box 68
Palm Harbor, Florida 34682

727 (813) 785-2148
727 (813) 787-3478
1-800-749-2207

A.N.A. Life Member #547

Printed in the United States of America

Table of Contents

Dedication

I would like to dedicate this book to:

My Lord and Savior, Jesus Christ...

The fabulous memory of my feisty mother, Rachel Elizabeth...

My late, good friend, Bob Rose of Renrob Coins...

To my sisters, Norma Williams and Waite Predmore
for their love and faith in me all these years...

To our children, Carlotta L. Bernard, Quinton B. Cline,
Carmellia J. Loyd and Keith A. Hyer...

To my wonderful wife, Vicki, for her unconditional love and loyalty. Vicki,
I dedicate this book to you with gratitude and my love.

Acknowledgements

I would like to acknowledge Michael Turoff of Flushing, New York for his provocative suggestion, many years ago, that there were two models who posed for Hermon A. MacNeil. This intriguing suggestion led to several conversations with the late Mrs. Hermon MacNeil and a visit to New Jersey to meet her. She contributed the newspaper article, pictures of Mrs. Irene MacDowell and a host of information, photos and clippings, etc. that verified the existence of two models and that MacNeil did indeed use a composite of both ladies for Miss Liberty.

I would also like to gratefully acknowledge the late Mrs. Cecilia MacNeil and her step-son Aldin MacNeil from California for their contribution of the medals, photos, etc.

My sweet wife, Vicki, has certainly stayed by my side throughout this revision, and I would like to acknowledge her efforts in typing, research, lay-out and assistance in getting this book to the publishers while she continued her full time work at the office.

About The Author

J.H. Cline has been a part of the numismatic world for over 40 years. Thirty-one of those years in Dayton, Ohio where he owned his store – Cline's Rare Coins on Salem Avenue. The last ten years he has been based in Palm Harbor, Florida with a suite of offices to serve his clients.

J.H. Cline is a life member of the American Numismatic Association, Indiana State Numismatic Association, Penn-Ohio Coin Clubs, Inc., National Silver Dollar Roundtable, Blue Ridge Numismatic Association, Inc., and Great Eastern Numismatic Association. He is an honorary life member of Greater Houston Coin Club and founded the Greene County Coin Club in Ohio many years ago. Memberships are also held with Central States Numismatic Society, Florida United Numismatists and numerous other organizations.

Standing Liberty Quarters are his specialty and he has given lectures at many national and regional coin conventions and at several of the local colleges and at the A.N.A. "Little Theaters" (or seminars, as they are now called). Many articles he has written have appeared in *Coin World, Numismatic News, Coins Magazine, The Numismatist* and *The Coin Dealer Newsletter.*

He is a regular contributor in the "A Guide Book of United States Coins" (the *Redbook),* "Handbook of United States Coins" (the *Bluebook*), and the "ANA Grading Standards for United States Coins." Over the years he has received awards for his mail order business and attends most major coin shows and auctions throughout the country. He has had a bourse table at each A.N.A. convention since 1970, with the exception of 1994.

J.H. Cline and Vicki A. Hyer were married in January of 1981 and have a composite family consisting of five children and numerous grandchildren. Vicki has worked full time in the business since the summer of 1978 and "holds down the fort" when Jay travels to the coin shows and auctions. She is truly his right-hand gal, or the "Gal Friday" in his offices. He found her when he ran a "Gal Friday" ad in the Dayton (Ohio) *Daily News.* She answered the ad and the rest is history.

My Visit To The Smithsonian

Reprinted from an article in the May 8, 1995 issue of *Coin World* titled, "Recent Visit to Smithsonian to Examine Standing Liberty Quarters Fun For Dealer"

I have visited the Smithsonian Institution several times over the years, taking my children to the various space exhibits, gem stone exhibits and, of course, the coin exhibits. (I began collecting coins in a serious way in 1953. Before that, my collection consisted of a few Buffalo nickels, Indian Head cents, Liberty Head nickels, and a small grouping of Barber coins in a cigar box.)

Jay Cline (left) meets Dr. Richard Doty, the curator in charge of U.S. Coins at the Smithsonian Institution.

Often I wished I could go "behind the scenes" and examine the Standing Liberty quarter dollars that I felt must be hidden back in the vaults of the National Numismatic Collection, but the opportunity never presented itself until late March, 1995.

The Smithsonian receives many requests regarding special viewing of certain items in a year's time, and I considered it a privilege when they agreed to allow Arnold Schwartz and me to examine the entire Standing Liberty quarter dollar collection. It was a dream come true!

Arnold had contacted me about three years ago by mail, and then arranged to meet with me in Chicago to talk about Standing Liberty quarters. We stayed in touch over the months and he worked very diligently to set up our Smithsonian visit.

It was with sheer ecstasy and delight that I walked into the National Museum of American History at the Smithsonian Institution in Washington, D.C., recently, and met Dr. Richard Doty, the curator in charge of United States coins.

Arnold and I had planned to be at the museum by 10 or 11 a.m., but my plane was late arriving, and the airline lost my luggage. We met Dr. Doty in the lobby — he was leaving for lunch. We stopped, got special visitor badges, and he invited us to join him for lunch. We had a great lunch and it gave us time to get acquainted and relax from the frustrations of running late. I determined

that I knew Dr. Doty from his past employment at the American Numismatic Society in New York and from American Numismatic Association conventions he occasionally attends.

I must say, it was certainly a thrill to be seated in the Numismatic Library of the National Numismatic Collection. Floor to ceiling (15-foot ceilings) shelves "stuffed" full of numismatic reference books from around the globe, but a certain Standing Liberty quarter book was absent from the collection. That matter was quickly remedied. I had brought a few copies with me and there are now two autographed copies on the shelves and in the archives.

Arnold and I started examining the Smithsonian's collection of Standing Liberty quarters at about 1 p.m. The greatest arrived first—the entire tray of Standing Liberty quarters from the vault was hand-delivered personally by Dr. Doty. The prize of the entire collection was on this tray — two pattern coins (Judd 1796-A, as cataloged in *United States Pattern, Experimental and Trial Pieces* by J. Hewitt Judd and Abe Kosoff)! It's the variety with the ribbons on the reverse and no stars or designer's initials. (For those familiar with my book, Standing Liberty Quarters, revised in 1986, it is the coin pictured on the back of the cover). The opportunity to see these two pieces made the trip worthwhile for Arnold and for me!

The first pattern coin has a light golden obverse and reverse with a Matte Proof finish (a bit more matte on the obverse than on the reverse), irregular surfaces and a different hair style than was on the adopted version. By "different" I mean there is no detail on Miss Liberty's hair — none of the curls appear around her forehead, nor do they appear in her hair from front to back. There is just a slight overlap of hair on top of her head all the way to the front. It is very much like the overlap on the reverse eagle's head. There is no definition at all, but I didn't mind. It is one of the famous patterns!

The sash across Miss Liberty's body is strong, but where it trails from her right hand it becomes incused rather than being raised as is the norm. The word LIBERTY on the obverse has somewhat flat letters, not well rounded on the top as would be expected. The reed and bead design is also somewhat flat from 11 o'clock to 3 o'clock, which does occur on some of the Standing Liberty quarters.

Regarding the stars on either side of Miss Liberty: The bottom two are strong, as are the top two, but not many of the others are strong. The middle stars are weak, which is characteristic of most 1916s.

There are no lines in the shield, neither vertical nor horizontal, and the inner shield is a bit irregular in design—not the perfect roundness as on the regular issue. The digits of the date look a bit rough with the 6 having an indication of retooling. There is a rather crude line under the date from about 5:30 o'clock to 7 o'clock, with the last reed on both sides of the date flat and about twice as broad as the normal reed and bead on the remainder of the coin.

The coin board I examined at the Smithsonian.

On the reverse, the first things to catch the eye are the prooflike fields: light golden with very reflective fields, including between the letters. This coin would impress the most astute collector.

The leaves on the branch have 14 berries on the right and 15 berries on the left. The last A in AMERICA has a crossbar that is nearly nonexistent—very faint. The eagle's breast is very boldly struck as are the wing feathers. The pin feathers were nearly nonexistent, but these small feathers on the leading edge of the eagle appear on very few pieces in the series, with the exception of the 1917 Bare Breast variety, which has a wire rim from about 7 to 11 o'clock. The obverse has almost a full wire rim.

The other pattern piece is somewhat less desirable in every respect: much lacking in prooflike fields and much more lightly struck. Both coils show doubling

of letters as well as the eagle's right wing.

The coins are two real beauties to behold. Each coin is probably Mint State 65, but one has a definite prooflike reverse!

We returned the next morning to view these gorgeous pieces again and to examine the pieces that are on display. The display pieces were removed (guarded all the way, of course) and brought into the library for examination.

Some of the more memorable pieces:

1916: Mint State 64 full head, light golden. Yes, a full head.

1917-S: Bare Breast MS-66 full head with a sharp full head and a beautiful prooflike reverse.

1918/7-S: is only an Extremely Fine 45 to About Uncirculated 50. No special traits on this one.

1919: is outstanding and is amazingly free of contact or "bag" marks. It has a lovely prooflike reverse, though not quite as nice as the 1927-D reverse. Once again, not quite a full head.

1927-D: looks deep mirror prooflike and has a frosty eagle, but it is not a full head.

1927-S: There are two pieces. The first is weakly struck and has no shield lines with about 70 to 80 percent head. Nice clean fields. Some die polishing can be seen on the obverse to the right of the shield and reverse die polishing between the eagle's wings and under his breast. The second piece is a very typical 1927-S in all respects; very softly struck from top to bottom.

Many of the pieces in the set are not full heads, but many pieces are virtually free of contact marks.

I would like to give a very special word of thanks to Dr. Doty, Jim Hughes, and Douglas Mudd of the National Numismatic Collection for the superior cooperation they gave us. If we expressed a need—from desiring a stereoscope, high sensor light, fluorescent light with magnification, extension cord, another coin tray —whatever we requested was granted quickly in a manner that could not have been nicer! Thanks a million! It certainly was nice to see a place where our government is doing a good job.

I mentioned that the airline lost my luggage. Within my suitcase was the photographic stand for my camera, along with the strobe lights, so I could not take photos of the coins. When the NNC staff discovered that I could not photograph the coins without my photographic stand, once again they came through with flying colors and very happily obliged me with the photos I desired.

For any collectors who are looking for a worthwhile tax write off, the Smithsonian's National Numismatic Collection could use some help in improving the Standing Liberty quarter dollar collection. The Smithsonian is in the middle of an austerity program, and the NNC has no money available to purchase much-needed pieces. With one of the finest gold collections in the world (if not THE finest), our NNC deserves a better exhibit of Standing Liberty quarters.

Every American should visit the Smithsonian Institution every three to five years. Please do not miss the coin exhibits located in the National Museum of American History. That area of exhibits, alone, is worth the trip to Washington, D.C.

Highlights of the Smithsonian Liberty Quarter Collection

1916 Pattern　　　　　　**1916 Pattern**

1917　　　　　　**1917-D**

1917-S **1919**

1920 **1921**

1924 **1927-S**

1928-D **1929-D**

Introduction: How I Got Started — And Other Stories

In 1953, at the National Cash Register Company in Dayton, Ohio I worked with a man named Kipp Carter. Kipp was an avid collector of coins, collecting mostly Indian Head cents and Lincoln cents. In circulation, he found a 1918-S Standing Liberty quarter and had cleaned it very aggressively (and it was very obvious - even to the untrained eye). Kipp offered it to me for the "whopping" price of 35¢! At the same time, I bought 3 1931-S Lincoln cents, CH BU at $7.00 each, for which my first wife left me, but she returned 2 days later. In those days it did not matter much that a coin had been cleaned or dipped (oops! There was no "dip" back then, only Brilliantine - a paste used with a Q-tip.) I took the coin in my hand and said "wow!" Look at the design on the inside of the rim (I know now to call it reed and bead). I proceeded to expound on this unusual design and the fact that it was not on any other U.S. coin, though the 1915 Panama Pacific $50 gold commemorative piece is close in design, but only in a fashion. They call it the "morse code" circle of long and short beads. When I asked Mr. Carter if he had ever seen a brand-new coin of this series, he stated that he had not, so I got out the Yellow Pages and let my fingers do the shopping and I found a coin shop. I use the term "coin shop" loosely, as it was a combination coin shop/book store with a dirty curtain separating the two sides. The other side of the store was a smut-book store - very smelly, etc. and was called Red's Book Store and Coins. (Long since gone out of business). Down 10 steps into the basement - a typical coin or book store for that time in Dayton, Ohio in 1953.

I went into the store and there was a man cleaning a Lincoln cent with Brilliantine. He did not stop when I entered, but continued his task, taking a cloth and wiping the paste off (probably leaving many lines). He then handed the coin to me and said "there, does that look great, or what?" Red had caused a medium grade VF-XF piece to look "new" and Red and was very proud of himself! Only then did he turn to me and ask if he could help me. I held out the polished 1918-S Standing Liberty Quarter and asked "do you have a new coin of this series?" He said that he had two pieces, but they were both type I. I did not know the difference and asked him to explain. He then handed me a raw one (not in a holder) and scolded me for not taking it by the rim! Since this was my first trip into a coin shop I had no idea how to hold a coin properly. He said that the Type I that I was looking at was the full nipple variety. I was looking at the spectacular head detail. Red then said "nobody cares about the head. Look at the full nipple". I must admit it was there.

Red had one at $5.00 that was not quite as well struck as the other. The better piece with full nipple was $7.50; a whopping 50% more than the other. I studied long and hard before shelling out that extra 50% for the same date and mintmark as the $5.00 piece. I finally traded in a roll of 1949-S and 1943-S Lincoln Cents (bank wrapped) for the $2.50 extra, and proudly took home my very first uncirculated Standing Liberty Quarter with a sharp, full head! This was probably a big mistake, because I then looked at all Standing Liberty Quarters expecting the same strike and strong full head to match the Type I piece I had purchased. I am very certain I would have purchased many other pieces if I had known that no other date or mintmark in the entire series has the nice, complete strike of the 1917 Type I's. I now know that whatever the series, the first year of issue is always the finest strikes. These first year of issue pieces are also the ones most often kept.

Thus began a lifelong endeavor. I loved the Standing Liberty Quarter series at first sight - and that love still burns white hot! I began to look for anything in print about the series, and found nothing. Even the Redbook only showed two grades: fine and uncirculated. The 1918/7-S was listed at $185.00 in uncirculated! There was a note at the beginning of the series stating that full head pieces, uncirculated, were worth up to 50% more. My 1917 Ty.I, purchased a week earlier, was listed at $3.50 and the 1916 was $100.00, uncirculated and $45.00, fine. This from the 6th Edition *"Guide Book of United States Coins"*, which covered 1953 and 1954 (due to lack of interest?)

I began to go through coins by the barrel. Once found a VF 1918/7-S. What a treat! Sold it to a dealer a few days later for $75.00 although the Redbook only listed it in Fine at $65.00. WOW!! I was sure on cloud 9 and well on my way to collecting Standing Liberty Quarters.

I won't bore you with all that happened over the next 40+ years, but it would probably fill several volumes. Wrote many articles on the series; two books; contributed to the *Redbook* and the *Bluebook*, and the *A.N.A. Grading Guide*. Before Walter Breen wrote his "Walter Breen's Encyclopedia of U.S. and Colonial Coins" he handed me his manuscript and asked me for any corrections in the Standing Liberty Quarter section before he turned it over to the publisher. I had only two. #1: There were no Federal proofs of the series, but a matte proof 1916 without designer's initials exists. #2: Full head Standing Liberty Quarters are achieved from new dies. (His theory was that non-full heads were the result of improper pressure on dies). He did not list me as a contributor, but when he autographed a copy to me, he wrote "not yet acknowledged contributor, 7/23/88 - Cinn. A.N.A."

Hope you enjoyed my ramblings. How much of 40+ years can you put into one article.

God Bless You,

J. H. Cline

Chapter 1

HERMON ATKINS MacNEIL

•

THE MAN

•

THE DESIGNER

This is a photograph of Hermon Atkins MacNeil, taken September, 1902; his age at the time was 36. Hermon took great pride in presenting himself at all times in a professional manner. This was also about the time he had competed his work on the 1901 Pan Pacific decoration for the Anthropological Building in Buffalo, New York.

Pictured here is Hermon Atkins MacNeil with his second wife, Cecila, whom Hermon married in the 1930's after his first wife, Carol, passed away. Though at the age of 60 his hair was thinning, his eyes still had that twinkle that was a trait of Hermon's character. At this age he was still participating in tennis and taking his morning strolls at the crack of dawn. Hermon enjoyed excellent health until his prostectomy operation in 1934. His excellent example of good health was an image of which he was very proud. Mr. MacNeil died in 1946 of natural causes.

Hermon Atkins MacNeil

Hermon Atkins MacNeil designed the series of Standing Liberty Quarters, it was only one of the many, many accomplishments he achieved in his life.

He was born February 27, 1866 in Prattville, Massachusetts, which at the time had not been named. Hermon grew up on his father's farm; he was one of five children. Hermon grew up feeding the chickens and milking the cows, hoeing the vegetable gardens and all the other chores that go with farm life. His farm home was a giant twelve-room house. His mother died when he was 13 years of age and his older sisters took care of him from that point on.

Hermon's first design or sculpture was when he was 11 years old. Coming home from school he stopped in a mud hole and began to make a head and fashion it out of the mud. After being laughed and poked at by all of his classmates he succeeded in finishing his first sculpture or design and then hurried home to tell his mother about it. She was very pleased with Hermon.

A favorite aunt of Hermon's, Lizzie, desired to give a cultured note to the education of her nieces and nephews. Lizzie obtained the services of a maiden lady to teach the children to draw, paint, and watercolor. Hermon, of course, was invited to attend this class which was held on Saturday afternoon, and he found himself extremely interested in this class and participated very actively. All of these lessons were held outside and only ran for a short period of time during the summer. In those days art or anything that pertained to the type of interest Hermon had in sculpture and artistic things were not taught in high school or certainly not taught in the high school that he attended, so whatever interest or cultivating interest he had in art, watercolor and whatever else, had to be motivated outside of high school.

Hermon's cousin, Jeannette Mitchell, attended an art school in Boston called the Boston State Normal Art School, now the Massachusetts School of Art, and invited Hermon to attend. He asked his father about it and his father said no because he saw no livelihood in it for him. He asked his high school principal for his opinion and he thought it was better to first finish high school. Hermon then turned to Jeanette's mother who was a very prosperous gem and seal engraver who encouraged him to attend. Hermon knew of one graduate of the school who was getting as much as $25.00 per week for mechanical drawing which was a marvelous

sum indeed. His father finally gave his consent. This, incidently, was a free school. The school was primarily for training teachers for drawing in the Massachusetts schools. The course was quite comprehensive, though it did present phases of mechanical drawings of all kinds, ship drafting, architecture, geometrics of all kinds as well as free hand charcoal, watercolor, oil painting, modeling, sculptures, and so forth for all the students.

When Hermon began in this school it was in the middle of the year and he had to work late at night to make up for the lost time. He passed the first year's work with credits and a great deal of eagerness. While attending this art school Hermon still had to tend to his farm chores. Hermon had to walk five miles to attend school because he lacked the ten cents it took for the horse car ride that ran from home to the school. After graduation ceremonies from this school he arrived home to find his first award for his four hard years of work; on the dining room table was a check for $100. This brought tears to Hermon's eyes because it was from his father who had worked overtime to make this gift available.

Immediately after finishing this school Hermon was offered and accepted a position to teach drawing at Sibley College at Cornell University. For his first year of service he received $750. However, he did such a great job the second year they raised his salary to $1000.

In 1886 Hermon felt that he needed to take a trip abroad to further his education, so the third year after graduation, by scraping and saving $500, he took leave of his teaching position. Going abroad he was instructed by a Dr. Robert H. Thurston that he should learn the French language. Hermon went directly to the Julienne Art School in Paris, France. There, Henri Scrapu, a sculptor, was his main professor and certainly was kind to him. Hermon was running out of funds so he asked his Uncle Henry Mitchell for $500.00 to further his studies. During one of the summers Hermon took a three week trip down through southwest France; which he paid for by making base relief busts at hotels he stopped at along the way. Hermon's first year at the Art Academy was free if he could pass the examinations. He was lucky being admitted sixth out of seventy five opponents. Throughout the year Hermon was also successful in winning other awards at the school competing among all of the other students. At the year's end he needed to pack and go back home to see his father, brothers and

Hermon MacNeil's beautiful, picturesque, College Point studio for a 47 year period of time. This housed a lifetime collection of complete sculptures; completed designs; partially completed works; some of Hermon's most treasured works — either in picture form or the original castings. Just a momentous amount of collection from trash to treasures.

Hermon's dwelling house with connecting breezeway to his studio. As much time as Hermon spent in his studio, it's hard to say which was his dwelling house. Frequently, Hermon would work into the wee hours of the morning completing a project that frequently was done for free. One of the more notable indebtednesses is the statue Hermon did of McKinley in the McKinley Park, Columbus, Ohio. According to the information that I have, there is still a balance of over $7,000 due.

Pictures do not do this justice. The upper portion of this picture or the loft area all around the ceiling had figures, castings and dust of every conceivable description; large, small and in between, of some of Hermon's works. Many of which, I am sad to say, ended up in the harbor waters. What a lost treasure!!

sisters.

When he arrived in New York City, St. Gaudens was the great sculptor of the time. Hermon went to him and he was kind enough to give him a letter to Phillip Martiny, another sculptor, who had done considerable work at that time designing sculptures for the up-and coming exposition at Chicago in 1892. He rather doubtfully took Hermon on as a helper. At the end of his first week he asked what he thought he should pay him; since he had no professional experience, he could set his own salary. Hermon was thinking he would be happy with only two or three dollars a day but Mr. Martiny asked if $5 would be enough. So, for the next year Hermon spent his time doing professional work and learned a great deal from Philip Martiny. The Worlds Fair was supposed to open in 1892 but because of a labor dispute the buildings were running behind schedule so it was put off until 1893. Incidently, his salary by that time was $8 a day.

Around 1894 Hermon took his first studio in Chicago, Illinois, to see if he could make it on his own. He was soon asked to teach evenings at the School of Art Institute at Chicago. Almost immediately he had four face reliefs to do of the life of Pierre Marquette.

In 1895 Hermon took a western trip with two of his friends, Hamlin Garland and C.F. Browne. This was the trip that would change and motivate Hermon's entire life as most of his works were Indian in nature and this trip would burn into his mind the direction that would follow him for the rest of his life in his designing, sculpture, etc. Denver and Cripple Creek, Colorado were the first stops on their trip and Hermon was very disappointed when there were no Indians. They then went on a 1000 mile trip through the mountains and gorges of Colorado via the Rio Grande Railroad then down towards the south via the Santa Fe. They spent a large amount of time in Arizona, New Mexico and Colorado where Hermon and his companions found plenty of Indians. Hermon stated that here he was so keenly interested that he thought he was in heaven. He flared to a high pitch working from daylight to dark modeling and casting the types and figures. He shipped the one-foot models back to Chicago in boxes for studying later. Hermon said his greatest thrill was the visit to the northwest corner of Arizona where the annual, famous prayer for rain was to take place on the top of the Mesa at Oraibi. To reach this Indian settlement it was necessary to travel 110 miles on horseback. This was called the snake dance, a religious-type ceremony, and the Indians that participated were of the Hopi Tribe. The ceremony took a total of nine days to complete. The eighth day was being celebrated underground where the rain dancers spent time with the

snakes. The snakes were not de-poisoned and included such poisonous ones as rattlers, moccasins and whatever others were found in this particular area. The Indians handled these snakes with a very small amount of fear. They practically went without eating during the whole nine days of ceremony. This also was the point that inspired Hermon to cast a medal as well as a sculpture of the Indians at this war dance carrying snakes in their mouths.

Upon their return from the Western trip, Mr. Browne and Mr. MacNeil took a studio in the Marquette Building in Chicago, and began some Indian sculptures and work on the material that both of them had made and shipped back. They no sooner got settled in their new quarters until Hermon MacNeil received a letter from New York asking him to send photos of his work. The reason for this was that there was a Rhinehart fund that was set up in Baltimore to be devoted to the development of young sculptors in America. This school was under the auspices of the American Academy in Rome. This scholarship was offered for one year to Mr. MacNeil who had a sudden fear that perhaps he would lose his Americanism by associating with the old European art. He finally did agree to accept the scholarship in Rome. It was necessary for Hermon to visit the Baltimore Committee that funded this particular scholarship which was headed by Gillman of the famous John Hopkins University. It was here that Mr. MacNeil met Carol Brooks, his first wife, whom he married a week before he left for Rome around Christmas time in 1895. Hermon spent from 1896 to 1900 in the Villa Aurora Art Department. The academy had rented the Villa Aurora in connection with the archeological school. Villa Aurora, which has a high terrace, beautiful garden, roses, marble floors and ceiling decorated to the highest degree of very able Italian taste, still stands today and is occupied by an Italian aristocrat. It was here that Hermon marketed his first work of art to the President of the Santa Fe Railroad, Mr. Edward E. Aier. He was shown the piece of the Running Indian that Hermon fashioned after the Indians at Mesa handling the snakes. He quickly priced the figure to Mr. Aier at $250; he bought ten pieces. The President of the United States, Theodore Roosevelt, visited Mr. MacNeil's studio in New York City in his absence and was very disappointed when he could not buy a copy of one of those Indian runners and President Roosevelt was so disappointed and angry that he slammed the door, practically knocking it off its hinges.

During the summer Hermon, as well as his associates, would make quite extensive trips throughout parts of Italy inspecting buildings, architectures, structural designs, etc. A lot of his evenings were spent with his wife bicycling, picnicking and so forth in the hills of Italy. Many times Hermon would do a sculpture in exchange for lodging and meals, so many pieces of his work rest in the hills of Italy.

His wife Carol was also an artist. She, too, developed a series of bronze figures of various household artifacts such as tea and coffee urns. Carol is best known for her work of art called "The Foolish Virgin" which she did for Mrs. Cyrus McCormick of Chicago.

Hermon also designed the Pan Pacific Exhibition medal for exhibitors and won the gold medal for the design.

Hermon continued to design, sculpt, and teach; first at the Pratt Institute, then at Art Students League and the National Academy of Design in College Point. He worked some forty odd years and achieved great acceptance and fame throughout the United States and the World. Hermon was also elected President of the American Sculptor Society. (An office he held for 22 years.)

On October 2, 1947, at 7:30 p.m. life left one of the world's greatest architects, designers, sculptors and modelist. So many things could be said about Hermon MacNeil. He led a full, satisfying life and left behind so much beautiful work.

Carol MacNeil with their two sons.

"The Foolish Virgin"

A Chafing-Dish by Mrs. MacNeil

"The Tear Drop" by Mrs. MacNeil

A Vase by Mrs. MacNeil

Medal of Honor — Architectural League of New York City
designed by and awarded to H.A. MacNeil.

Poppenhusen Institute Commemorative Medal, 1918.

Pan American Peace Medal, 1901.

Hopi Indian Prayer for Rain, 1889.

Hermon A. MacNeil's Best-Known Works

The Following is a list of MacNeil's best-known works, their locations and dates of completion (when known).

Primitive Chant, 1891-93, statue, 2 versions, 8 copies. 4 bas-reliefs for the Marquette Building in Chicago, 1890-95.

"Agnese Mattelia" portrait bust sculpted in Rome, 1895-1898.

From Chaos Came the Dawn, relief sculpture, 1895-1900.

The Sun Vow, statue, 1898.

Hopi Runner, bronze statuette, 1899.

Hopi Prayer for Rain, sculpted in Rome, exhibited at Metropolitan Museum of Art in 1899.

In Ambush, 1896-1900, no copies.

Pedimental decorations for Anthropological Building at Pan-American Exposition at Buffalo, 1901.

Despotic Age, grouping for U.S. Government building at Buffalo Exposition, 1901.

Eastern pediment, U.S. Supreme Court building, Washington, D.C.

Gold Medal struck in celebration of Buffalo Exposition.

Exhibit of 22 works at Pratt Institute, 1902, 17 of which were Indian subjects.

Dancing Greek Figure, statuette, 1902.

Zephyr, statuette, 1902.

Decorative sculptures for St. Louis Fair of 1904.

McKinley Memorial, portrait statue, 1900-1905, for Columbus, Ohio.

The Coming of the White Man, grouping done for the City of Portland, Ore., 1905.

United States Quarter, 1916, known as Liberty Standing Quarter.

Ezra Cornell, portrait statue, campus of Cornell University, Ithaca, N.Y., 1915-1917.

Angel of Peace, 1918, Flushing, L.l.

Judge Burke Memorial, portrait statue done for the city of Seattle, Wash.

Judge Ellsworth, portrait statue done for city of Hartford, Conn.

General George Rodgers Clark, portrait statue for temple in Vincennes, Ind.

Into the Unknown, marble, Brookgreen Gardens.

Senator O.H. Platt, bronze high-relief portrait in Hartford, Conn.

Statue of General George Washington for Washington Arch in New York City, 1918.

Pilgrim Mother and Pilgrim Father, (or Pilgrim Fathers) memorial bronze figures located in Waterbury, Conn.

Pere Marquette, portrait statue, done for Chicago's West Park, 1926.

4 War Memorials in Albany, N.Y., Whitinsville, Mass., Flushing, N.Y. (1925), and Philadelphia.

Bas-relief frieze done for Missouri State Capitol, 1920's.

Defenders of Fort Sumpter, memorial grouping done for Charleston, S.C., in 1932.

Intellectual Development and Physical Development, companion groupings for Poter Gymnasium at Northwestern University.

Dr. Elmer E. Brown, portrait bust located at New York University, 1933.

John Stewart Kennedy, portrait bust located at New York City Public Library. 1933.

Pony Express, statue, located at St. Joseph, Mo., 1940.

Portrait busts of Roger Williams, James Monroe, Frances Parkman, Rufus Choate, for New York University Hall of Fame.

Hermon Atkins MacNeil, Sculptor

OBITUARY (Source Unknown):

Hermon Atkins MacNeil, eighty-one, American sculptor who designed the 25 cent piece bearing the standard figure of Liberty and whose works include the statue of General George Washington at the base of the Washington Arch in Washington Square, died Thursday at his home at 121-01 Fifth Avenue, College Point, Queens.

Mr. MacNeil, whose career as a sculptor extended from the 1890's to the early 1940's, specialized in American Indian and pioneer subjects for memorials and public buildings in cities throughout the United States. He also executed busts of famous Americans and did design work for buildings at the Chicago World's Fair in 1893, the Paris Exposition in 1900, the Pan American Exposition in Buffalo in 1901 and the Panama Pacific Exposition in San Francisco in 1915.

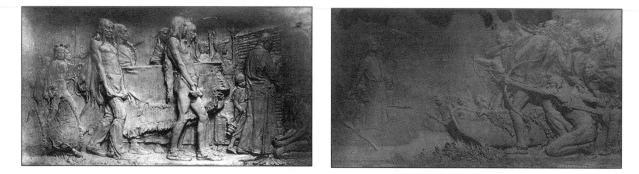

Indian Burial reliefs. Two of four burial reliefs Hermon MacNeil did for the Marquette Building in Illinois. The most famous of the four is the "Indian Burial of Pere Marquette" shown above left.

Burial reliefs Hermon MacNeil did for the Marquette Building in Illinois.

Mr. MacNeil won a competition in which fifty artists participated for the design of the quarter, which was accepted by the United States Government in 1916. The coin is no longer minted; in 1932 it was replaced by the Washington Quarter. On the coin's obverse side the figure of Liberty descends a flight of steps in an attitude of welcome, holding a laurel branch of peace in one hand and a shield in the other. Mr. MacNeil's signature, a Roman "M", is visible just to the right of the date on the obverse side. The reverse side shows an eagle in flight.

Born in Chelsea, Mass., the sculptor was the son of John Clinton MacNeil, a farmer and house builder, and Mary Lash MacNeil. He studied at the Massachusetts Normal Art School in Boston and then went to Paris, where he was a pupil of the French sculptor Chapu at the Julian Academy and of Faguierre, at the Ecole des Beaux-Arts. He continued his studies in Rome after receiving the four year Roman Rinehart Scholarship in 1896. There he became a favorite pupil of American sculptor John Quincy Adams Ward.

The following is reprinted from the *New York Herald Tribune*, October 4, 1947.

Mr. MacNeil opened a studio in College Point in 1900 which became his home and workshop for forty-seven years. There he conceived the statues "Sun Vow" and "Primitive Chant" owned by the Metropolitan Museum of Art, the McKinley Memorial at Columbus, Ohio; "Coming of White Men" at Portland, Ore.; "Pony Express," St. Joseph, Mo.; the statue of General George Rogers Clark, Vincennes, Ind.; the war memorial in Flushing Park, Flushing Queens; the Marquette Memorial in Chicago; "The Pilgrim Fathers" in Waterbury, Conn.; General Washington's statue and other works.

He executed the busts of Rufus Choate, Roger

Internal Photos of Hermon's workshop.

Mr. MacNeil's latest completed work, The McKinley Monument, dedicated at Columbus, Ohio.

Williams, Francis Parkman and James Monroe for the Hall of Fame at New York University and a bust of his teacher and early sponsor, Mr. Ward, for the Hall of Artists at New York University.

Mr. MacNeil's works won medals at the Chicago, Buffalo, Paris, and San Francisco expositions as well as at the exposition at Charleston, S. C., in 1902, the St. Louis Exposition in 1904, and the Atlanta Exposition, Atlanta, Ga., in 1895. He was a president of the National Sculpture Society and a member of the National Academy of Design, the New York Architectural League, the New York Municipal Art Association, the American Federation of Arts, the National Academy of Arts and Letters, the American Academy in Rome and Century Association.

Mr. MacNeil's first wife, Mrs. Carol Brooks MacNeil died in 1944. In 1946 he married Mrs. Cecilia W. Muench. He also had two sons, Claude L. and Alden B. MacNeil, and a half sister, Miss Helen MacNeil.

East pediment of the Supreme Court Building, Washington, D.C. One of Hermon's works that he was most proud of depicting our three departments of justice: Executive, Legislative and Judicial. With the flair in style of the ancient Romans and Egyptians close scrutiny reveals a fascimilation of the reverse of the Mercury dime that was issued the same year as Hermon's quarter.

HISTORY

The process of selecting the new design was enacted into law and approved September 26, 1890, under authority of Section 3510, of the U.S. Rev. Stats.

THE YEAR 1915

In the beginning of 1915 the coinage of the U. S. was about to make a change at the request of the President. For the first time in history the quarter would be different from the dime and the half dollar.

There were three new coins to make their debut in 1916. The new winged Mercury Dime, the Walking Liberty Half; these two having been designed by A. Weinman, and the Standing Liberty Quarter designed by Hermon A. MacNeil. A renaissance of interest in United States silver coins was beginning.

THE AMERICAN INSTITUTE OF ARCHITECTS
The Octagon, 1741 New York Avenue
Washington D.C.

June 4, 1928.

My dear Mr. McNeil:

Acting for the Secretary, I take pleasure in writing to advise you of your election as an Honorary Member of The American Institute of Architects - at the Sixty-first Convention of the Institute, held in May.

A certificate of election has been sent to you under separate cover.

As an Honorary Member you will receive, complimentary, The Journal of The American Institute of Architects, its Year Book, and the Proceedings of its annual Conventions.

Sincerely yours,

Executive Secretary.

Mr. Hermon A. McNeil,
679 Northern Boulevard,
College Point, L. I., N. Y.

X-G

P.S. - Would appreciate it if you would please advise if your address, as shown, is the one to which you desire the Journal, and other communications, sent.

Chapter 2

GOVERNMENT BUREAUCRACY

THE WHITE HOUSE
WASHINGTON

August 17, 191_.

My dear Sir:

Congress has passed an act of which I enclose
a copy. Under the second section it becomes my
duty to secure a gold medal of the kind described
in the act. At the suggestion of the Commission
of Fine Arts I write to ask if you will not under-
take to furnish designs for the obverse and reverse
of such a medal.

I have asked several other artists to do the
same thing, and the designs will be submitted to
the Commission of Fine Arts at Washington for the
purpose of determining which one should be selected.

I hope you will think it worth while to take part
in this competition. You will note that the total
amount allowed is only One Thousand Dollars, so that
the artist's compensation must necessarily be small.

Sincerely yours,

Wm H Taft

H. A. MacNeil, Esquire,
    College Point, L.I., N.Y.

Enclosure

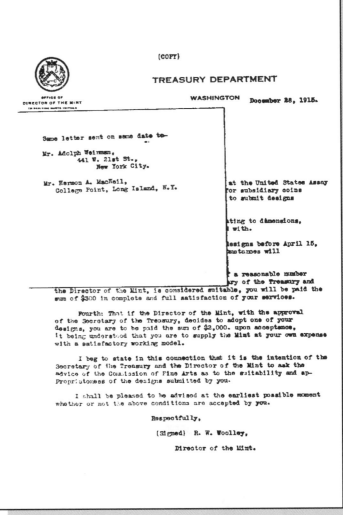

(COPY)

TREASURY DEPARTMENT

OFFICE OF
DIRECTOR OF THE MINT
IN REPLYING QUOTE INITIALS

WASHINGTON   December 28, 1915.

Same letter sent on same date to—

Mr. Adolph Weinman,
    441 W. 21st St.,
    New York City.

Mr. Hermon A. MacNeil,
    College Point, Long Island, N.Y.

                                    at the United States Assay
                                    for subsidiary coins
                                    to submit designs

                                    ating to dimensions,
                                    with.

                                    esigns before April 15,
                                    mstances will

                                    a reasonable number
                            ry of the Treasury and
the Director of the Mint, is considered suitable, you will be paid the
sum of $300 in complete and full satisfaction of your services.

        Fourth: That if the Director of the Mint, with the approval
of the Secretary of the Treasury, decides to adopt one of your
designs, you are to be paid the sum of $2,000. upon acceptance,
it being understood that you are to supply the Mint at your own expense
with a satisfactory working model.

        I beg to state in this connection that it is the intention of the
Secretary of the Treasury and the Director of the Mint to ask the
advice of the Commission of Fine Arts as to the suitability and ap-
propriateness of the designs submitted by you.

        I shall be pleased to be advised at the earliest possible moment
whether or not the above conditions are accepted by you.

                Respectfully,

                (Signed) R. W. Woolley,

                            Director of the Mint.

TEL 47 - FLUSHING
HERMON A. MAC NEIL
NORTHERN BOULEVARD
COLLEGE POINT
NEW YORK

Jan. 4th, 1916.

Mr. R.W. Wooley,
   Director of the Mint
   Washington, D.C.

Dear Sir:-

      I beg to acknowledge your kind favor of December 28th., commissioning me to submit designs for subsidiary coins of the United States under stipulated conditions.

      In our conversation in New York regarding the matter I felt we left the subject somewhat vague on certain points. your letter now in hand,on which,still leaves me somewhat uncertain.

      Let me say first that I had a very pleasant visit at the Mint last week and beleive I have a very clear understanding of the necessities of coin designing through the courtesy of Messrs. Barber and Morgan, who were very cordial indeed. Amongst other information Mr. Barber, gave me a typewritten copy of the law regarding coin designing which reads:-" Sec. 18. Devices and legends upon coins. Revised Statues, 3517. Inscription. That upon the coins of the United States there shall be the following devices and legends: Upon one side there shall be an impression emblematic of liberty, with an inscription of the word "Liberty" and the year of the coinage, and upon the reverse shall be the figure or representation of an eagle, with the inscriptions "United States of America" and "E Pluribus Unum" and a designation of the value of the coin, and inscription,"In God We Trust?"

In looking over the subsidiary coins in use, I find the twenty-five and fifty cent pieces are the only coins that entirely conform to this law. The reverse of the other coins have no eagle as the law directs.

      In conversation with you I gathered your intention was to allow as much freedom as possible in the new designs. In your letter the first condition reads: "that all requirements of law relating to dimensions, designs, devices and legends shall be complied with." In wording, date and value of coinage, I presume this law must be adhered to, but with "Liberty" may we give a broad interpretation of the word and is it obligatory to use the eagle , on the reverse.

      In the matter of submission of designs, you name April 15th., as the limit and that there shall be several of them. These conditions, Mr. Wooley, lead me to think that you may be somewhat unfamiliar with the method of producing and work necessary to fulfill them. It is not unusual for a sculptor in an important work to make a number of sketches, that to him indicate sufficiently what the ultimate result would be of the thought expressed, but to others might easily be meaningless, but in the process of elimination he generally settles down to one or two that he would develope further before submitting for approval.

      The privilege of submitting more than one design

TEL 47 – FLUSHING
HERMON A. MAC NEIL
NORTHERN BOULEVARD
COLLEGE POINT
NEW YORK
-3-

might perhaps be left to the sculptors particularly as I
understand your intention is not to use more than one design ^{obverse & reve}
from each and also your sum of THREE HUNDRED ($300.) DOLLARS
if none are used is a very inadequate one for the several
designs called for.

Do you mean April 15th., as the date of your selection
of designs or of the completed work of the sculptor? Further,
I still feel you are making considerable of a competition in the
conditions you offer,(which I infer are similarly made to the
other two sculptors), without the usual and necessary conditions
that make a logical competition.

I am confident you will understand this letter is not
made in the spirit of fault finding. My object is to understand
as clearly as possible the conditions of your kind offer to
submit these designs. In the meantime, please beleive me,

Very sincerely yours,

H. A. mac neil

Jan 13/16

TEL 47 – FLUSHING
HERMON A. MAC NEIL
NORTHERN BOULEVARD
COLLEGE POINT
NEW YORK

Jan. 11th, 1916.

Mr. R. W. Wooley,
Director of the Mint
Washington, D.C.

Dear Sir:-

In response to your kind offer commissioning me to
submit designs for the subsidiary coins of the United States
under conditions contained in your letter of December 28th.,
and of January 6th. I beg herewith to accept the same and
shall do my best to try and produce something that shall be of
use to you. I realize the far reaching value of a good design
on coins that are in the hands of our entire population.

On account of the very limited time in which you
allow for these designs, I have consulted with Mr. Weinman and
Mr. Polasek in regard to the best method of proceedure and we
have mutually agreed to try and have such preliminary sketches
or studies for these designs as we have made, ready on or about
the middle of March so that by your having them all together
at the same time your judgement of their merits may be facilitated
and as little time as possible lost in making it. This will
leave an extremely short time for the development of such designs
as may be chosen and I trust that you will find it possible for th
greater perfection of such designs, to add to April 15th., such time
as you may find necessary to use in making your decision of the
preliminary sketches upon which we are already at work.

In the meantime, please beleive me,

Very sincerely yours, *H.A.macneil*

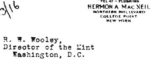

TEL 47 - FLUSHING
HERMON A. MacNEIL
NORTHERN BOULEVARD
COLLEGE POINT
NEW YORK

Feb. 7th, 1916.

Hon. R. W. Wooley,
    Director of the Mint
        Washington, D.C.

Dear Sir:-

            Referring to may last letter to you, I find that I
made an error in saying that the three sculptors you chose for
making the designs for the subsidiary coins would have their
preliminary designs in shape about the middle of March, I should
have said about the middle of February, as we will need considerable
time for carrying out such designs as may be accepted.

            Recently meeting the other two sculptors we have
decided that we can probably all three forward our material to you
so as to arrive in Washington by the 21st, of this month at the
earliest.   Should you find however that no action could be taken
on them on that date or for some days after, it would be convenient
if you would kindly let us know and advise us what dates after
the 21st, it would be desirable for these sketches of the three
sculptors" to be at your office.

            Very respectfully yours,

                    H A MacNeil

(COPY)

TREASURY DEPARTMENT

OFFICE OF
DIRECTOR OF THE MINT
IN REPLYING QUOTE INITIALS

WASHINGTON   February 28, 1916.

Mr. Hermon A. MacNeil,

        College Point, New York.

Dear Mr.MacNeil:

            It gives me pleasure to notify you informally that
the Secretary of the Treasury and I have accepted one of your models
for the obverse of the quarter dollar. In other words, you have been
awarded one-half design out of a possible three designs.

            Your models will be returned to you Saturday next. I wish
to do the Fine Arts Commission the courtesy of showing them what were
submitted, and the models selected.

            Of course, the contents of this letter are to be treated as
confidential until such time as the Secretary of the Treasury and the
Director of the Mint decide to make the awards public.

                    Respectfully,

                    (Sg) R. W. Woolley,

                            Director of the Mint.

Obverse and reverse of one of the first designs submitted by MacNeil. This coin existed in plaster of Paris only. Most likely part of the "debris" that was hauled to the bay at the dismantling of Hermon's studio in 1948.

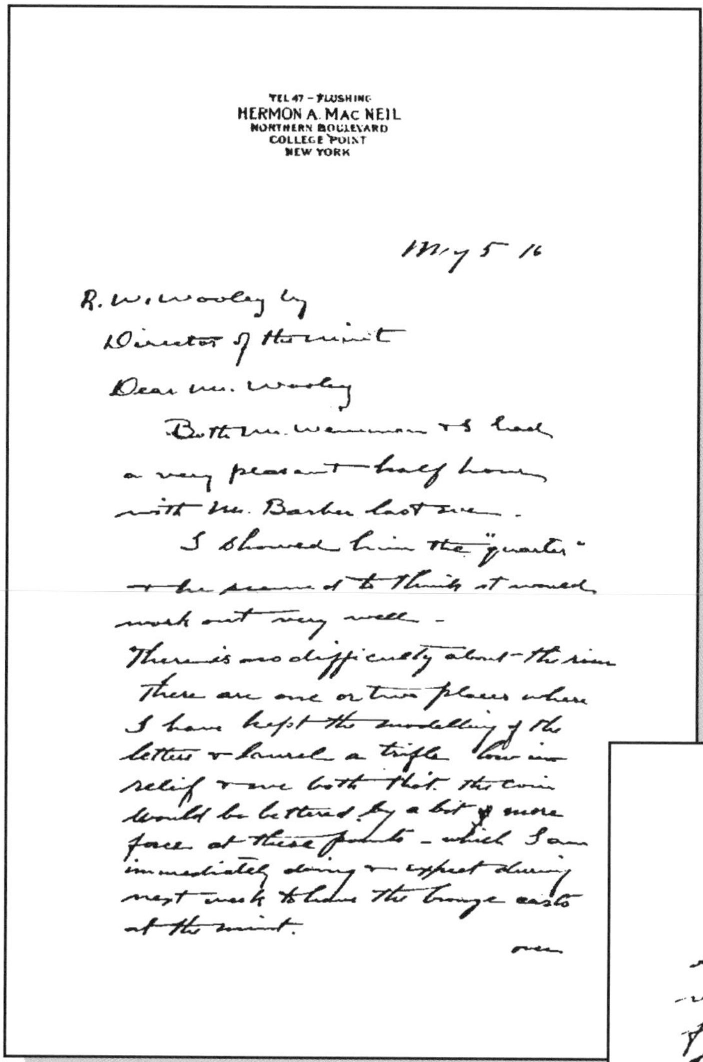

TEL 47 – FLUSHING
HERMON A. MAC NEIL
NORTHERN BOULEVARD
COLLEGE POINT
NEW YORK

May 5 16

R. W. Wooley Esq
Director of the Mint

Dear Mr. Wooley

Both Mr. Weinman & I had a very pleasant half hour with Mr. Barber last eve.

I showed him the "quarter" & he seemed to think it would work out very well.

There is no difficulty about the rim. There are one or two places where I have kept the modelling of the letters & laurel a trifle low in relief & we both think the coin would be bettered by a bit of more face at these points – which I am immediately doing & expect during next week to have the bronze casts at the mint.

over

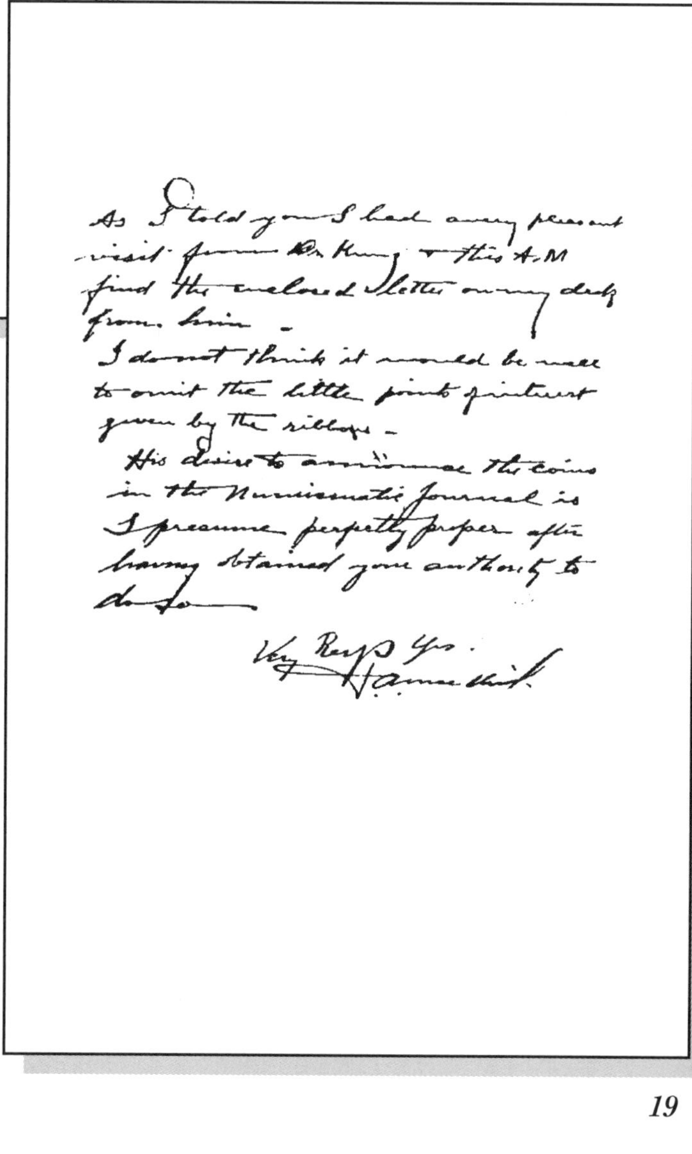

As I told you I had a very pleasant visit from Dr. Kunz & this A.M find the enclosed letter on my desk from him.

I do not think it would be well to omit the little point picturesque given by the ribbons.

His desire to announce the coins in the Numismatic Journal is I presume perfectly proper after having obtained your authority to do so.

Very Resp Yrs.
H. A. MacNeil

TREASURY DEPARTMENT

WASHINGTON

OFFICE OF
DIRECTOR OF THE MINT

May 23, 1916.

Mr. Hermon A. MacNeil,
  Northern Boulevard,
    College Point, New York.

Dear Mr. MacNeil:

It gives me pleasure to notify you
formally that the designs submitted by
you for the proposed new Quarter Dollar
have been accepted, and are hereby approved.

Very truly yours,

R. W. Woolley

Director of the Mint.

Approved:

Wm. G. McAdoo

Secretary.

Copy + photo to
Phila. aug 7/16.

August 19, 1916.

Mr. Hermon A. MacNeil,
  Northern Boulevard,
    College Point, N. Y.

Dear Sir: -

Replying to your letter of August 16th instant,
I hereby approve the modified design for the obverse
of the new twenty-five cent coin, photograph of which
you submitted for my inspection.

I take pleasure in granting you permission to
place your initials on the new quarter-dollar, pro-
vided the letters are small in design and are placed
on an inconspicuous part of the coin, as is the case
in connection with coins now in circulation.

Sincerely yours,

TREASURY DEPARTMENT

WASHINGTON

OFFICE OF
DIRECTOR OF THE MINT
IN REPLYING QUOTE INITIALS

June 7, 1916.

Mr. Hermon A. MacNeil,
    Northern Boulevard,
        College Point, N.Y.

Dear Sir:

        I beg to acknowledge the receipt of your letter of the 7th instant
relative to presenting a silvered copy of the plaster model of the accepted
design for the proposed new quarter dollar. Replying, I beg to say that the
law would not permit you to make any use whatever of the model, in any material
or form. The provisions of Sec. 169, Penal Code, explicitly prohibit the use
of the design, which is now the property of the Government.

                Respectfully,

                    (Sg) F. H. Chaffin,

                        Acting Director of the Mint.

TEL 47 – FLUSHING
HERMON A. MAC NEIL
NORTHERN BOULEVARD
COLLEGE POINT
NEW YORK

Aug 13 – '7.

R. S. Baker Esq.
    Director of the Mint
        Washington D.C.

Dear Sir –

        I was much pleased to
get your announcement
that the Quarter Dollar
is lawfully back on an
artistic basis. It is now
being minted.

        While I want to thank
both you & the Secretary
for the friendly interest in
this matter at this time —

        Thank you also for the
sample which I shall
look for with interest —

            Ever Sincerely [signature]

(COPY)

TREASURY DEPARTMENT

WASHINGTON August 19, 1916.

Mr. Hermon A. MacNeil,
    Northern Boulevard,
        College Point, N. Y.

Dear Sir:

    Replying to your letter of the 16th instant, I hereby approve the modified design for the obverse of the new twenty-five cent coin, photograph of which you submitted for my inspection.

    I take pleasure in granting you permission to place your initials on the new quarter dollar, provided the letters are small in design and are placed on an inconspicuous part of the coin, as is the case with the coins now in circulation.

        Sincerely yours,

        (Sg) Wm. G. McAdoo,

           Secretary.

        Bureau of the Mint, August 29, 1916.

Respectfully referred to the Superintendent, U.S. Mint, Philadelphia, for his information. Mr. MacNeil has this day been instructed to submit to this Bureau a photograph of the quarter dollar showing the position and relative size of the initials he proposes to place upon the coin. You will be advised when the same is approved.

        (Sg) F. H. Chaffin,

           Acting Director of the Mint.

HERMON A. MAC NEIL
NORTHERN BOULEVARD
COLLEGE POINT
NEW YORK

Aug. 31st, 1916.

Mr. F. H. Chaffin,
  Acting Director of the Mint, Treasury Dept.
    Washington, D. C.

Dear Sir:-

    Enclosed please find according to your request the photograph of the Obverse of the new TWENTY-FIVE CENT PIECE with two places indicated for my signature. I have used the monogram (M.M.) in both places, but it is possible that (M) alone would be better for this signature on account of the very diminutive size. It is possible also that the spot under the head of the dolphin on the right would be the better place as I should then make it merely an incised letter. The size indicated is the size, approximately, of Frazer's Five Cent Piece and will be practically unseen except for the magnifying glass.

    Immediately on receipt of your O.K. of this detail, I will have the bronze cast made and forwarded to the Mint.

        Very respectfully yours,

(COPY)

TREASURY DEPARTMENT

WASHINGTON

September 1, 1916.

Superintendent, U. S. Mint,

    Philadelphia, Penna.

Sir:

    I beg to advise you that Mr. Hermon A. MacNeil has this day been authorized to place his initial or initials on the quarter Dollar of his design. The signature is to be placed under the head of the dolphin on the right of the coin.

    The sculptor has been requested to hasten as much as possible the preparation of the cast of the obverse of the coin.

               Respectfully,

               (Sg) F. J. H. von Engelken,

               Director of the Mint.

NOTE: Mr. MacNeil's initial M appears in the design as struck by the Mint on the obverse, to the right of the foot of Liberty.

This is the very first design by Hermon MacNeil for the quarter. Miss Liberty is topless, as she was from the very beginning. When the original design was about to be changed to the type 2 design, Secretary W.G. McAdoo states in the last paragraph of his petition (see 1st Session, 65th Congress Report No.78 on page 32), "…the artist has found that they were not true to the original design and that a great improvement can be made in the artistic value and appearance of the coin by making the slight changes the act contemplates…"

Nothing could be further from the truth! The truth is that they wanted to cover Miss Liberty's bust, as the Congressmen's wives were opposed to the bare breasts. They called it everything else.

MacNeil was opposed to the changes and the following letter bears this out, as do several throughout this book. Charles Barber ("conservative Barber," as he was known) could not wait to get his two-cents worth in resulting in spoiling the artistic beauty of the Type 1 Standing Liberty Quarter.

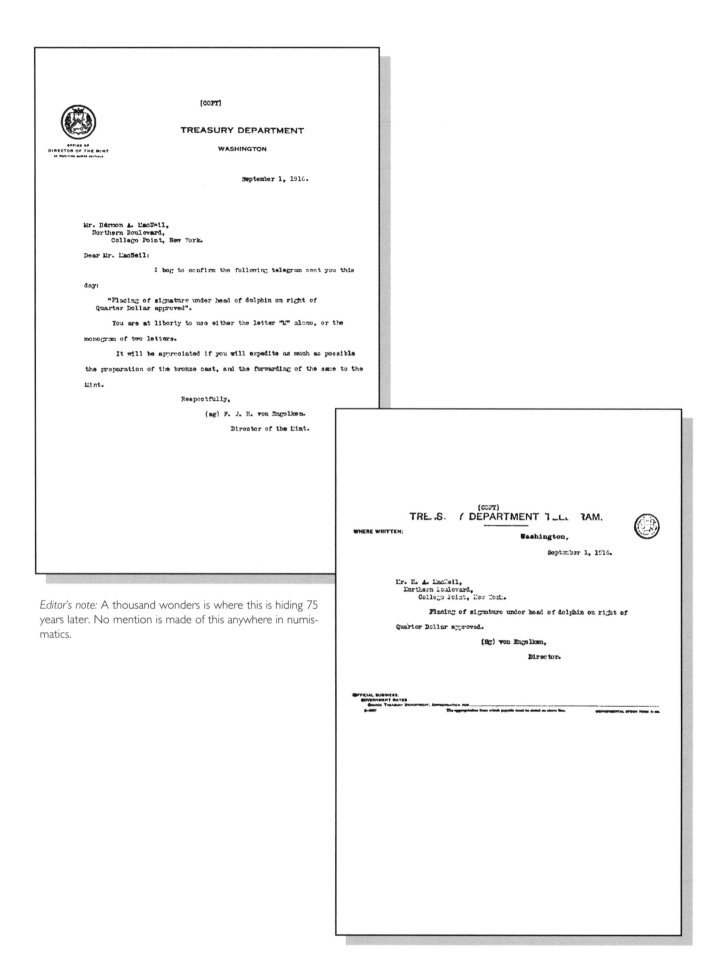

(COPY)

TREASURY DEPARTMENT

WASHINGTON

September 1, 1916.

Mr. Hermon A. MacNeil,
    Northern Boulevard,
        College Point, New York.

Dear Mr. MacNeil:

I beg to confirm the following telegram sent you this day:

"Placing of signature under head of dolphin on right of Quarter Dollar approved".

You are at liberty to use either the letter "M" alone, or the monogram of two letters.

It will be appreciated if you will expedite as much as possible the preparation of the bronze cast, and the forwarding of the same to the Mint.

Respectfully,

(sg) F. J. H. von Engelken.

Director of the Mint.

Editor's note: A thousand wonders is where this is hiding 75 years later. No mention is made of this anywhere in numismatics.

(COPY)

TRE.S. / DEPARTMENT T L. RAM.

WHERE WRITTEN:

Washington,

September 1, 1916.

Mr. H. A. MacNeil,
    Northern Boulevard,
        College Point, New York.

Placing of signature under head of dolphin on right of Quarter Dollar approved.

(Sg) von Engelken,

Director.

OFFICIAL BUSINESS.
GOVERNMENT RATES.

September 6, 1916.

Dear Mr. Secretary:

In response to your request for a memorandum about the new coins, I send you herewith a letter from the Director of the Mint and one from Assistant Secretary Malburn.

The mechanical difficulty seems to be due to the fact that the relief of the designs is too high to make a perfect coin. You will note that Mr. von Engelken says that if you should decide to use the low relief it would be necessary either to have the artist provide new plates or to let the designer at the mint work up the artist's patterns into one that will conform to the mechanical requirements of the mint.

Faithfully yours,

M Cooks

The Honorable
    The Secretary of the Treasury.

September 6th, 1916.

Director of the Mint.
    Washington, D. C.
Dear Sir:-

Referring to the proposition of the model of the new Quarter Dollar, the work is already in the caster's hands and I expect to be able to send the completed bronze before the end of the week, to Mr. Barber at Philadelphia.

In the production of the dies, the former director of the Mint, Mr. Wooley, was anxious to have the coins left as they came from the sculptor's hands, without rubbing or burnishing on the background of the dies and so far as we can see, there is no reason why this should not be done, although, Mr. Barber seems always very anxious to rub down the background as much as possible which gives the coin a very unpleasant and metallic look.

It would be a great pleasure to me and I am sure also to Mr. Weinman, if you find yourself in accordance with this point of view and if so, would instruct the engraver to carefully follow it.

Very respectfully yours,

H.A. MacNeil

new Design

MINT OF THE UNITED STATES AT PHILADELPHIA.

SUPERINTENDENT'S OFFICE.

October 13, 1916

Subject: Lead impressions new design quarter enc.

The Director of the Mint,
   Washington, D. C.

Sir:

I am enclosing under separate cover lead impressions of the die for the new design quarter dollar, changed in accordance with your instructions received upon the occasion of my last visit in Washington.

Kindly signify your O.K., or desired correction. Upon receipt of the same, we will promptly proceed with the execution.

Respectfully,

Superintendent.

MINT OF THE UNITED STATES AT PHILADELPHIA,

SUPERINTENDENT'S OFFICE.

REGISTER.

October 20, 1916

Subject: New design quarter dollar.

The Director of the Mint,
        Washington, D.C.

Sir:

I have the honor to submit in accordance with
your request sample impressions of the new design of
the twenty-five cent piece in the enclosed envelopes,
numbered as follows:

#1 Contains a silver impression in place of the
lead one previously submitted for the purpose
of comparison of the softening of the lettering
of the same.

#2 Is a finished piece consisting of the original
submitted models of the artist.

#3 Is a finished piece embodying the suggestions
received from you upon the occasion of your last
visit, the natural luster having been taken off
for the purpose of ready comparison with the
sample coin first submitted.

#4 Contains a sample piece in appearance and
luster as will be the natural product of the
press.

Mr. MacNeil called on the telephone, requesting
the privilege of coming to Philadelphia for the purpose
of being made acquainted with the progress made with

Mint U.S. at Philadelphia.

(2)

the design as submitted by him.

Awaiting your decision in the matter, I am,

Respectfully yours,

J. M. Joyce
Superintendent.

(4 encs.)

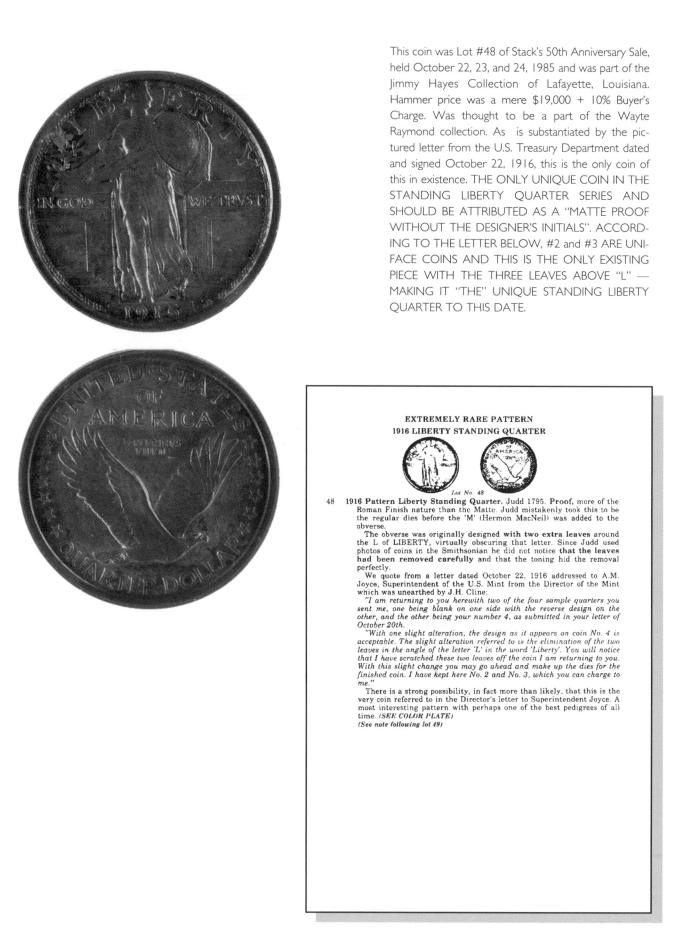

This coin was Lot #48 of Stack's 50th Anniversary Sale, held October 22, 23, and 24, 1985 and was part of the Jimmy Hayes Collection of Lafayette, Louisiana. Hammer price was a mere $19,000 + 10% Buyer's Charge. Was thought to be a part of the Wayte Raymond collection. As is substantiated by the pictured letter from the U.S. Treasury Department dated and signed October 22, 1916, this is the only coin of this in existence. THE ONLY UNIQUE COIN IN THE STANDING LIBERTY QUARTER SERIES AND SHOULD BE ATTRIBUTED AS A "MATTE PROOF WITHOUT THE DESIGNER'S INITIALS". ACCORDING TO THE LETTER BELOW, #2 and #3 ARE UNIFACE COINS AND THIS IS THE ONLY EXISTING PIECE WITH THE THREE LEAVES ABOVE "L" — MAKING IT "THE" UNIQUE STANDING LIBERTY QUARTER TO THIS DATE.

EXTREMELY RARE PATTERN
1916 LIBERTY STANDING QUARTER

Lot No. 48

48   **1916 Pattern Liberty Standing Quarter.** Judd 1795. **Proof,** more of the Roman Finish nature than the Matte. Judd mistakenly took this to be the regular dies before the 'M' (Hermon MacNeil) was added to the obverse.

The obverse was originally designed **with two extra leaves** around the L of LIBERTY, virtually obscuring that letter. Since Judd used photos of coins in the Smithsonian he did not notice **that the leaves had been removed carefully** and that the toning hid the removal perfectly.

We quote from a letter dated October 22, 1916 addressed to A.M. Joyce, Superintendent of the U.S. Mint from the Director of the Mint which was unearthed by J.H. Cline:

"I am returning to you herewith two of the four sample quarters you sent me, one being blank on one side with the reverse design on the other, and the other being your number 4, as submitted in your letter of October 20th.

"With one slight alteration, the design as it appears on coin No. 4 is acceptable. The slight alteration referred to is the elimination of the two leaves in the angle of the letter 'L' in the word 'Liberty'. You will notice that I have scratched these two leaves off the coin I am returning to you. With this slight change you may go ahead and make up the dies for the finished coin. I have kept here No. 2 and No. 3, which you can charge to me."

There is a strong possibility, in fact more than likely, that this is the very coin referred to in the Director's letter to Superintendent Joyce. A most interesting pattern with perhaps one of the best pedigrees of all time. *(SEE COLOR PLATE)*
(See note following lot 49)

OFFICE OF
DIRECTOR OF THE MINT
IN REPLYING QUOTE INITIALS

TREASURY DEPARTMENT

WASHINGTON

October 22, 1916.

Dear Mr. Joyce:

I am returning to you herewith two of the four sample quarters you sent me, one being blank on one side with the reverse design on the other, and the other being your number 4, as submitted in your letter of October 20th.

With one slight alteration, the design as it appears on coin No. 4 is acceptable. The slight alteration referred to is the elimination of the two leaves in the angle of the letter "L" in the word "Liberty". You will notice that I have scratched these two leaves off the coin I am returning to you. With this slight change you may go ahead and make up the dies for the finished coin. I have kept here No. 2 and No. 3, which you can charge to me.

Very truly yours,

Director of the Mint.

Hon. A. M. Joyce,
Superintendent, U. S. Mint,
Philadelphia, Penna.

OFFICE OF
DIRECTOR OF THE MINT
IN REPLYING QUOTE INITIALS

TREASURY DEPARTMENT

WASHINGTON

November 11, 1916.

SUBJECT: New Design Quarter Dollar.

Dear Mr. Joyce:

I have just had word from the Secretary that he would like to have the figure of "Liberty" on the obverse side of the Quarter Dollar brought out more clearly. I told him that I thought we could not do this without consuming a great deal of time and going over all of our past work again. He, therefore, agreed to let the Quarter go as it is. I told him, however, that we decided to sharpen the design of the shield, and I hope you can do this before sending out the dies.

Respectfully,

Director of the Mint.

Hon. A. M. Joyce,
Superintendent, U. S. Mint,
Philadelphia, Pa.

Jan. 11, 1917.

Hon. J. H. Engleken,
Director of the Mint,
Washington.

Dear Sir:-

Yesterday I learned from some sample quarters sent me that work on the new coins had been resumed at the Mint. As these coins received had a resemblance to the design I had first made last Spring but had later changed and modified considerably with the full approval of the then Director, Mr. W. P. Wooley, as well as the Secretary of the Treasury and which I had every reason to believe would be coined you can imagine my surprise. I immediately visited the Mint and was still more surprised and interested to see the many variations that had already been tried on this coin, many of them arrangments that I myself had already tried and discarded. It is evident, Mr. Von Engelken, that you and the Department you represent as well as myself are all trying for the same thing, namely the best coin possible.

Since receiving the approval of and sending to the Mint the last model I have repeatedly written and even telephoned the Supt. asking to see the progress and to be of any possible use. The coins just received are the first intimation I have had that work had been going on.

Having looked it over carefully I am of the opinion that some of the features of the first discarded design which you now retain in this one are good. Yet, while I have great respect for the opinion and point of view of yourself and the Secretary of the Treasury as the final judges, I am sure you will permit me as the sculptor to incorporate in this your apparently final decision certain changes that while leaving the coin as now planned will enormously improve it from an artistic point of view. It is this for which, as I understand it, the sculptor was employed.

These modifications on the obverse are as follows:-
1. To bring the head of the figure a trifle lower so as not to appear to be holding up the rim of the coin.
2. To prevent the figure appearing "bowlegged".
3. To minimize the sagging of the covering of the shield by having it pulled a little tighter.

These three improvements are shown on my later model and appear to me to be absolutely essential.

I should also like to see the letters of the word Liberty slightly smaller but I like them flat as now shown on the coin.

Don Taxay, The U.S. Mint and Coinage states: "MacNeil wrote to the Mint Director, Von Engelken on January 11, 1917, asking permission to alter the design on the Quarter. This interesting letter cannot be located." However, here is not only a copy of that letter but also a photo of the coin with changes. Still no mention is made of the mail covering for Miss Liberty.

Obverse and Reverse of Type 2 Silver Quarter Dollar.

#2

On the reverse by soiling one of the coins, as it will become in use, you will notice that the eagle has been dropped so low as to make it appear that the tail connects with the lettering below. I presume your intention was to disengage the feather of the wing from partly covering the A of America, a feature which I personally liked. It would be a simple matter, however, to make the "OF" take less room and thus raise all the letters above the bird a trifle. By placing the bird at the bottom of the coin it gives the appearance of a low flying (or just rising) eagle in which case the position of the talons as they now are would be wrong.

From my study for this bird I am convinced that the talons are extended behind only when well under way at a reasonably high altitude.

I trust in these changes which I am asking you to make, Mr. Von Engelken, you will see both regard for your own point of view, as well as reasonableness also from my own and I ask for them with the more assurance as my name and reputation as an artist is already connected with this coin and my initial upon it.

With high consideration, I am,

Very truly yours,

H. A. MacNeil

TEL 47 – FLUSHING
HERMON A. MAC NEIL
NORTHERN BOULEVARD
COLLEGE POINT
NEW YORK

Hon. J. H. Von Engleken
Director of the Mint

Dear Mr. Von Engleken –

Reporting my pleasant interview at the Mint with the Supt. Mr. Joyce. It was agreed that they would take the obverse + keep the design practically as now issued merely substituting the second modeling of the figure for the present one. This will give practically the same figure except that it will be a bit more resonant + purposeful + solidly constructed. Very much like it.

difference between a good + bad egg superficially about the same – but when you look into it, very different –

The reverse – I have in hand + expect by Sat. afternoon or Sunday to have the 5" model in shape – In fact I have three arrangements of the same elements now used any one of which I am confident is a great improvement –

With the thot. that by chance you might be in N.Y.C. I am now writing – Should you be here Sat. or Monday I will be found on the phone 367 Gramercy – on Sunday at 47 – Flushing – I should like to show them to you if convenient –

Very Respectfully,
H. A. MacNeil

TREASURY DEPARTMENT

WASHINGTON

April 5, 1917.

The Honorable
The Secretary of the Treasury.

Sir:

I have the honor to submit for your consideration a draft of an act to authorize the alteration of the designs of the present Quarter-Dollar in accordance with a specimen submitted by Mr. Hermon A. MacNeil, the sculptor whose designs were accepted May 23, 1916, for the Quarter-Dollar now being issued.

The modifications proposed are slight, the principal one being that the eagle has been raised and three of the stars placed beneath the eagle. On the reverse the lettering has been re-arranged and the collision with the pinions of the wings obviated. These changes, together with a slight concavity, will produce a coin materially improved in artistic merit, and not interfere in any way with its practical use.

Respectfully,

Director of the Mint.

MODIFICATIONS OF THE DESIGNS OF THE CURRENT QUARTER DOLLAR.

JUNE 13, 1917.—Committee of the Whole House on the state of the Union and ordered to be printed.

Mr. ASHBROOK, from the Committee on Coinage, Weights, and Measures, submitted the following

REPORT

[To accompany H. R. 3548.]

The Committee on Coinage, Weights, and Measures, to whom was referred H. R. 3548, providing for the modification of the designs of the current quarter dollar, having had the same under consideration unanimously instructed the chairman to report the bill to the House with the recommendation that the bill be passed.

The object of the bill is set forth in the following letter from the Secretary of the Treasury to the chairman of the Committee on Coinage, Weights, and Measures:

TREASURY DEPARTMENT,
OFFICE OF THE SECRETARY,
Washington, April 16, 1917.

MY DEAR CONGRESSMAN: I have the honor to submit for your consideration a draft of an act to authorize the modification of the designs of the current quarter dollar in accordance with a specimen submitted by Mr. Hermon A. MacNeil, the sculptor whose designs were accepted May 23, 1916, for the quarter dollar now being issued.

The modifications proposed are slight, the principal one being that the eagle has been raised and three of the stars placed beneath the eagle. On the reverse the lettering has been rearranged and the collision with the pinions of the wings obviated. These changes together with a slight concavity, will produce a coin materially improved in artistic merit, and not interfere in any way with its practical use.

I am sorry to have to ask for this change, but since the original dies were made the artist has found that they were not true to the original design and that a great improvement can be made in the artistic value and appearance of the coin by making the slight changes the act contemplates. I take the liberty of proposing a form of bill which will accomplish the object if enacted by the Congress, and heartily recommend its passage.

Sincerely, yours,

W. G. McADOO,
Secretary.

Hon. WILLIAM A. ASHBROOK.

QUOTES WITHOUT COMMENT

Regarding a query as to a "mar on some 1919-D quarters", M. Vernon Sheldon has this to say: "The rim 'defect' is not a defect at all but a variety. It is due to a chipped collar used when this part was struck. This is certainly is not a defect; but should be classified as a variety".

DESIGN OF THE QUARTER

The coin pictured here is one of the designs that Hermon Atkins MacNeil presented to the Treasury Department for acceptance when the contest was on. The one pictured is very similar to the Standing Liberty Quarter; having two dolphins and Roman Numeral writing for Hermon's initial both to the right of the shield and under the dolphin on the right. This photo convinces your author that Miss Irene MacDowell is indeed the lady who posed for this particular piece, if not all of the Standing Liberty designs. It does appear that Mr. MacNeil took parts of the two models to complete the design on the Standing Liberty Quarter. This coin was apparently never produced in metal or at least if it was, it was destroyed by the mint and certainly would be a beautiful piece in a patterned coin. However, there is no proof that any of these do exist and having personally talked to Mrs. Hermon MacNeil and her son, Aldin MacNeil, from California, both assured your author that none of these are in existence in metal, that they were cast in a type of plaster-paris for presentation to the Treasury Department or minting secretary for acceptance or rejection.

THE LAW GOVERNING THE DESIGN

A government report states that the design was "intended to typify in a measure the awakening interest of the country to its own protection". In the new design, Liberty is shown as a full-length figure, front view, with head turned toward the left, stepping forward to the gateway of the country, and on the wall are inscribed the words "In God We Trust". The left arm of the figure of Liberty is upraised, bearing the shield in the attitude of protection, from which the covering is being drawn. The right hand bears the olive branch of peace. On the field above the head is inscribed the word "Liberty", and on the step under her feet, "1916". In the design on the obverse there is materialistic design and beauty, more of the things this country stands for than any coin designed before or since. It conveys the meaning as clearly as any written word can do: "O.K.", "Peace", or "War". Take it or leave it, we are ready for either. The reverse of the coin necessitates by law a representation of the American Eagle, and is here shown in full flight, with wings extended, sweeping across the coin. The inscriptions on the reverse are: "United States of America", "E. Pluribus Unum" and "Quarter Dollar" below. Connecting the lettering on the outer circle are thirteen stars.

It is interesting to note that the number of rivets on the shield of Type I is thirty and the number of rivets on Type 11 is sixteen. Also, the reed and bead design has been flattened, wide spaced and in general, rougher, less artistic. More of the shield Miss Liberty is holding is showing in Type I than Type 11 and is considered by most to have lost most of its fine art design which was intended to portray the finest example of adult womanhood.

ABOUT THE DESIGN

The Standing Liberty Quarter was coined by order of President Theodore Roosevelt, since he and his aides said the Barber Quarter (coined since 1892) did not meet the artistic designs that our foreign neighbors were using. After listening to competent advisors they concluded that there should be a new design. Many competing artists and sculptors had submitted many designs and changes; subject of course, to federal laws and regulations concerning U.S. coinage. The best design submitted would be accepted for striking. At this time the ground work was laid for the redesigning of three pieces of our minor coinage.

However, not until March 3, 1916, did the press dispatch out of Washington, D. C., mention any contemplated change in our present coinage system. Treasury officials maintained "they had no available information on the subject". However, the press and coin periodicals kept up a steady stream of hot rumors about a coinage change. Nothing was made public until the annual report of the Director of the Mint that was released in January of 1917. At that time, the new half dollar, quarter and dime information was released along with illustrations of all specimens. Examples were publicly exhibited in New York by the American Numismatic Society, courtesy of the United States Treasury Department. The mint report said Hermon A. MacNeil was the designer of the new quarter. The design on the obverse typifies in a measure the awakening interest of this country's own protection. However, this design (reed and bead) goes back to the ancient Greek and Roman architecture which exemplifies Mr. MacNeil's background, which is Bohemian. In the design of the reverse Mr. MacNeil tried to capture the majesty of the American Bald Eagle in its glorious flight. However, many thought he failed; many claimed it had the wings of an eagle and the body of a dove and the beak of a hawk. Others view this Eagle in flight as a better pro-portioned coin than any other United States coin.

According to British heraldry and the United States War Department Heraldic Section, the Eagle on the Standing Liberty Quarter is shown incorrectly. This Eagle flies to its left and the Eagle should always be shown flying or facing the dexter or honorable side, or to its right.

THE LAW

The law specified that on the obverse of the coin not only the word "Liberty" but a representation of Liberty shall be shown. In the new design, Liberty is shown as a full-length figure, front view, with head turned toward the left, stepping forward to the gateway of the country, and on the wall are inscribed the words "In God We Trust" which, also appears on the new half dollar.

The left arm of the figure of Liberty is up-raised, bearing the shield in the attitude of protection, from which the covering is being drawn. The right hand bears the olive branch of Peace. On the field above the head is inscribed the word "Liberty" and on the step under her feet is the date. The reverse of this coin necessitates by law a representation of the American Bald Eagle, which is shown here in full flight, with wings extended, sweeping across the coin. The inscriptions "United States of America" and "E. Pluribus Unum" and "Quarter Dollar" are also on the reverse. Connecting the lettering above the outer circle are 13 stars.

THE GREAT CONTROVERSY

With the new liberation of the American woman you would have thought the American people would be ready for uncovering some of the things that have not been uncovered; especially having had to look at the ultra conservative Barber design on all dimes, quarters, and halves for the past twenty four years. But women were still the "protected species" and that is why it came as such a shock to the nation that the United States Government would release a coin, according to the critics, as "obscene". No one, least of all the United States Government, intended to create an obscene coin. After all, artists were requested to submit their ideas but the final selections were made by a joint decision of the Treasury and the Commission of Fine Arts. A. A. Weinman had been selected for the dime and half dollar and Hermon A. MacNeil had been selected for the quarter. When the coinage change was first introduced the mint director, Mr. Woolley, was delighted since this was the first time in the history of our coinage that the quarter would not be like the dime and half dollar. This coin was unique in that it was intended to typify, in a small measure at least, the awakening interest of the country to its own protection.

There is a second controversy or "cover up" (no pun intended). When the senators' wives and representatives' wives objected to the bare-breasted Miss Liberty on the quarter, the requests to change the design were worded in every conceivable way. i.e.: would not stack properly; artistically incorrect; the design had lots of nooks and crevices and would catch a lot of germs; mint could not strike up the design on the obverse as mechanical requirements were incorrect; the eagle's feet were even wrong! Anything and everything except a written request to cover Miss Liberty's exposed breasts.

Mr. Farran Zerbe then wrote: "The most noticeable difference is on the reverse. The eagle is higher and there is a new arrangement of the stars, three stars being placed below the eagle. On the obverse the feathers of the head of Liberty are stronger. The sprig in her hand does not engage the "L". There are fewer dots in the shield, and the undraped chaste bust of the old has been given what looks like a corsage of mail." "A comparison of the old with the new pieces will convince collectors that an improvement has been made. The only serious objection to the old reverse was that the eagle was too low, which has not been raised to the center of the coin."

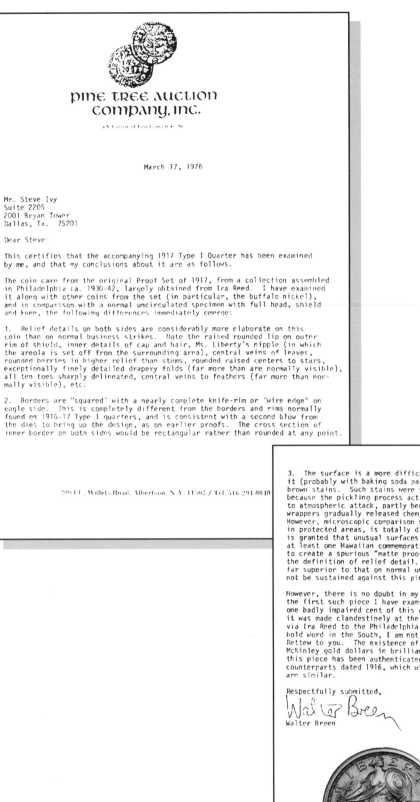

PINE TREE AUCTION COMPANY, INC.

A Subsidiary of First Coinvestors, Inc.

March 17, 1976

Mr. Steve Ivy
Suite 2205
2001 Bryan Tower
Dallas, Tx. 75201

Dear Steve:

This certifies that the accompanying 1917 Type I Quarter has been examined by me, and that my conclusions about it are as follows.

The coin came from the original Proof Set of 1917, from a collection assembled in Philadelphia ca. 1930-42, largely obtained from Ira Reed. I have examined it along with other coins from the set (in particular, the buffalo nickel), and in comparison with a normal uncirculated specimen with full head, shield and knee, the following differences immediately emerge:

1. Relief details on both sides are considerably more elaborate on this coin than on normal business strikes. Note the raised rounded lip on outer rim of shield, inner details of cap and hair, Ms. Liberty's nipple (in which the areola is set off from the surrounding area), central veins of leaves, rounded berries in higher relief than stems, rounded raised centers to stars, exceptionally finely detailed drapery folds (far more than are normally visible), all ten toes sharply delineated, central veins to feathers (far more than normally visible), etc.

2. Borders are "squared" with a nearly complete knife-rim or "wire edge" on eagle side. This is completely different from the borders and rims normally found on 1916-17 Type I quarters, and is consistent with a second blow from the dies to bring up the design, as on earlier proofs. The cross section of inner border on both sides would be rectangular rather than rounded at any point.

299 E.L. Willets Road, Albertson, N.Y. 11507 / Tel. 516-294-0010

3. The surface is a more difficult proposition, because someone cleaned it (probably with baking soda paste) in an attempt to efface black or dark brown stains. Such stains were virtually inevitable on matte proofs, partly because the pickling process activated the metal and made it more subject to atmospheric attack, partly because the cheap sulfite paper used in mint wrappers gradually released chemical contaminants which caused the tarnish. However, microscopic comparison shows that the underlying surface, especially in protected areas, is totally different from ordinary mint bloom. Now it is granted that unusual surfaces can be manufactured to order (I have seen at least one Hawaiian commemorative half dollar altered in surface this way to create a spurious "matte proof"), but such treatment invariably impairs the definition of relief detail. In the present coin, relief detail is so far superior to that on normal uncirculated specimens that such a claim could not be sustained against this piece.

However, there is no doubt in my mind that the coin is in fact a matte proof, the first such piece I have examined (compared to two 50¢, two 5¢ nickels, and one badly impaired cent of this date), and under the circumstances I conclude that it was made clandestinely at the mint for some VIP from whose holdings it went via Ira Reed to the Philadelphia collector (whose name, though long a household word in the South, I am not at liberty to disclose), finally through Joel Rettew to you. The existence of such proofs was suspected after the two 1917 McKinley gold dollars in brilliant proof state showed up about 1956. Now that this piece has been authenticated, others will probably follow, along with their counterparts dated 1916, which will be of value for comparison as the surfaces are similar.

Respectfully submitted,

Walter Breen

1917 Matte Proof Standing Liberty Quarter

This coin was Lot #1131 in the "Bowers & Merena" auction for the estate of Abe Kosoff on November 4, 5 and 6, 1985, where it was described as follows: (description courtesy of Bowers & Merena)

"1916 Pattern quarter dollar. J-1796a. 95.3 grains. Reeded edge. Silver Extremely Fine-40, polished.

An interesting pattern which differs in several respects from that finally adopted. The obverse, the design of Hermon MacNeil, features a full figure of Liberty, with head turned to the left, stepping through a gateway; the left arm upraised, bearing a shield from which the covering is being drawn; an olive branch in the right hand. LIBERTY is in the field above, and IN GOD WE TRUST is on the parapet, with 1916 on the step below her feet. Unlike the regular issue, there is no M on the base of the right portal.

The reverse differs considerably from the regular 1916 issue and has the flying eagle placed higher in the filed, and, notably, to the right and left has ornate lower branches with ribbons below, rather that the later adopted stars.

An exceedingly rare issue; just two or three specimens are believed to exist. The desirability of the 1916 pattern is enhanced by he 1916 date, for regular issues are highly prized in their own right. A classic which should draw wide bidding interest."

Hammer price was $5,800 + 10% Buyer's Charge.

Now known to be one of three pieces, this one owned by your author and two pieces in the Smithsonian's Collection, that have been examined by your author. No others are known to be in existence at this time.

Chapter 3

THE MODELS

Miss Doris Doscher, who is said to have posed for the Standing Liberty Quarter, was thirty-three years old at the time she modeled for Mr. MacNeil. She had successfully overcome a bout with polio as a child and at the time she was to have posed, she was a trained nurse.

Miss Doscher also posed for other leading sculptors of the time, namely: Daniel Chester French's "Memory", Hartley's "Kneeling Madonna" and Mr. Beech's "The Sculptor's Dream". Some of the better known are "Faith, Hope and Charity" in Washington, D. C.; "Diana and the Chase" at New York Metropolitan Museum of Art; "The Angel of Peace", part of the Flushing New York Memorial on Northern Blvd., and "Abundance", the central figure in the Fountain in front of New York's Plaza Hotel.

Miss Doscher (who became Mrs. Baum after marrying Dr. Wm. Baum) also was the first to present a health and beauty program. Her radio show on WOR ran daily, and her column and radio program continued until the demise of The World War.

She also starred in several silent movies. Twenty-four years ago, at the request of Mayor Lindsay, she participated in ceremonies renaming a 28 acre park in College Point, the Hermon A. MacNeil Park.

The same MacNeil, a sculptor, created a statue, "The Angel of Peace", for which Mrs. Baum posed. The statue is in the Flushing Memorial in front of the Armory on Northern Boulevard.

"Abundance", a statue which is the central figure in the fountain on 59th Street in front of the Hotel Plaza in Manhattan, was another for which Mrs. Baum posed.

Other statues she modeled for are "Faith, Hope and Charity", in Washington, D. C., "Diana of the Chase" in the Metropolitan Museum of Art, D. C., French's "Memory"; Hartley's "Kneeling Madonna" and Beech's "The Sculptor's."

Her influence as a columnist resulted in the New York City Board of Education naming her to its staff of lecturers for adult education classes. Mrs. Baum did her last public writing on health for *The American Vegetarian Hygienist,* a magazine, and the American Better Health publication. During those years she aided in organizing the Golden Age Clubs and appeared on several national T.V. programs.

For more than 50 years she was an active member of the Women's Press Club of New York City. She was past matron of the Order of Eastern Star. As president of the Women's Auxiliary of the American Naturpathic Association, Mrs. Baum also lectured at national conventions.

WERE THERE TWO MODELS???

Not until 1972 was Mrs. Doris Doscher Baum's status as the model for the Standing Liberty Quarter challenged. At that time, a 92 year old friend and associate, namely Mrs. Irene MacDowell, intimated to her family and only closest of friends that she indeed did model for the Standing Liberty Quarter. It was her beautiful statuesque figure that inspired Hermon Atkins MacNeil to design a coin that sent women into shock, children giggling and pointing, and men taking a second look at the exposed bust on the newly designed quarter. However, this must be taken in the beauty and art that the designer and model intended. Mrs. MacNeil describes Mrs. MacDowell "as a very respected and charming person and of the highest reputation". She had been a former broadway actress and the wife of a tennis partner of Mr. MacNeil. This was one of the closest guarded and best kept secrets of the 20th century. Mrs. MacNeil did not learn of this until after the death of Irene MacDowell on January 3, 1973. On January 4, 1973, Mrs. MacDowell's daughter, Louise MacDowell Wagner, wrote to Mrs. MacNeil and here are a few excerpts from that letter: "My mother was a very handsome woman, very statuesque, and both she and her friend Lula Funke, another family friend of the MacNeils, used to frequently pose for Hermon. I always knew she was the girl on the quarter." She also posed for some of the figures on the Soldiers and Sailors Monument in Albany, New York.

Miss Doris Doscher, her stage name Miss Doris Doree, as she did some acting on Broadway, modeled for other artists as well as Mr. MacNeil, and was one of the models that was used in the design of the Standing Liberty quarter. She was also a friend of the MacNeil family. A long time friend and tennis partner. Many interesting chapters could be written about Miss Doris Doscher and her association with the MacNeil family.

DORIS DOSCHER BAUM, "MISS LIBERTY" DIES AT 88

Services for Mrs. Doris Doscher (Miss Liberty) Baum, 88 of Whitestone, beauty and health columnist who was the model for the Liberty Quarter, will be held tomorrow at 10:00 A. M., in the Martin A. Gleason Funeral Home of Whitestone. Burial will be in Brookside Cemetery, Englewood, N.J.

Mrs. Baum lived at 10-27 147th St. She died Monday from complications after an accident six weeks ago when she fell and suffered a broken pelvis.

Prior to her journalist career she modeled about the turn of the century for the famous artists and sculptors of her time. She was chosen by Hermon A. MacNeil to pose for the Liberty Quarter and became known worldwide as "Miss Liberty"

Mrs. Baum, a lecturer, actress, counselor and confidant to millions, is credited with being the first health and beauty columnist in the newspaper field. She was born in Manhattan. As a young girl she had a back accident. Doctors said she would never recover from the illness which followed.

Determination and special exercises not only saved her life but inspired her to help others. She began her daily column, "Beauty, Health, Physical Culture and Psychology" in The New York World in the late '20's.

She also did feature articles on the health "secrets" of the celebrities of that era.

She leaves her husband, Dr. H. William Baum, a physiotherapist and chiropractor; a daughter, Mrs. Miriam Kiriluk of Farmingdale, and seven grandchildren.

MRS. IRENE MACDOWELL

Less than four months before she died an article appeared in "The Evening News", Newburgh, New York, on Tuesday, September 19, 1972. The article, written by Robert Curran, carries almost a full page article of Mrs. MacDowell finally admitting to being the "barebreasted" beauty that posed for her friend, Hermon MacNeil and that she posed a total of ten days before the sculptor achieved the ultimate perfection of the design he would enter in the contest and challenge the other artists and would be victorious with his design. In the article she also describes that clothing as a white, sheet-like drapery. Your author has a full length (color) picture of Miss Doris Doscher in a white, sheet-like attire which was the cover photo for the "Physical Culture Magazine" in 1920. Also, in the same issue was an article about and written by Miss Doscher.

Mrs. Irene MacDowell, the wife of Hermon's tennis partner, was also an ex-broadway actress. She was a very good friend of the MacNeil family enjoying many boat outings with them as well as attending the same church and living in the same community. She was very much a part of the life of Hermon and his family. According to Mrs. MacDowell's own statements some four (4) months before she died, she was one of the models who posed for Hermon Atkins MacNeil, a total of ten (10) days for the Standing Liberty Quarter. This did not meet with the approval of her husband and all parties involved concluded the credit should go to Miss Doris Doscher to keep from creating any problems in the families' relationship that might have a bad image on future generations.

Her Face Launched a Million Coins

By ROBERT CURRAN

NEW WINDSOR — The Liberty Girl, whose beautiful face and figure adorned United States quarters minted from 1916 to 1932, is alive and well at 92 years of age and still believes America is the grandest country of all.

Mrs. Irene MacDowell, who posed for the 25-cent piece 56 years ago, maintains an avid interest in world events but points out that contemporary women's liberation doesn't interest her.

For years the Liberty Girl symbolized peace and freedom in a growing America. Of the United States today she says: "In spite of all the talk you can't find another country that has the liberty we have. I think we're very lucky to be Americans."

The Liberty Quarter shows Mrs. MacDowell as the Liberty Girl descending a flight of steps. She is holding a laurel branch of peace in one hand and a shield in the other.

She posed for 10 days for sculptor Hermon A. MacNeil, who competed with 50 other artists seeking to design the 25-cent piece.

At the time, Mrs. Mac-Dowell, a former Broadway actress, wore white, sheet-like drapery and she described her dress for the quarter as "a kind of classical robe." She joked that she was fully dressed.

The coin was minted during President Woodrow Wilson's term.

MacNeil, one of the country's leading sculptors, i n c l u d e d Mrs. MacDowell as the Liberty Girl in a memorial statue. Mrs. MacDowell believes that the statue is now in Albany.

The famous Liberty Girl is an alert and remarkably lucid conversationalist today, who likes to watch television late at night and read t h e newspapers to keep up with what's happening.

She lives in a spacious New Windsor country home not far from Newburgh with her husband George, 90, daughter Louise and son-in-law, Harry Wagner.

Mrs. MacDowell has a strong love of her country and its

MRS. IRENE MACDOWELL
. . . with quarter she adorns

traditional stance of liberty.

"Some of the young don't feel that way but they don't know what it's all about. I guess they're trying to find their way," she comments.

No one except her friends and relatives ever knew that she was the person who posed for the Liberty Quarter, because no articles on the national level ever appeared about her.

The Liberty Girl believes clean country living is one of the reasons for her good health.

One flaw in the well-known,

teristic of the coin is the beautiful woman on it, Mrs. MacDowell.

The Liberty Girl has some feelings on Stewart Airport, which is not far from her.

The Metropolitan Transportation Authority (MTA) has condemned some 8,600 acres to act as a noise buffer zone for the airport's expansion, and the state may make Stewart into a major jet facility, one of the largest in the United States.

Of the airport land condemnation the Liberty Girl stated: "It's awful. You'd think it was Russia."

Do times change? Mrs. MacDowell joked that at the time she posed for the famous

quarter, a shopper could buy a pound of steak for 25 cents — a far cry from today's prices.

In 1932, the United States stopped minting its Liberty Quarter and it was replaced by the Washington Quarter. Occasionally, the old silver coin turns up in a cash register and in someone's pocket and is often stored away for safekeeping.

Meanwhile, like the coin, history and ideology, The Liberty Girl continues.

Photographs by Robert Demery

artistically-designed quarter of which she is so prominent a part, is that it wears easily. The piece is somewhat difficult to find in the exchange of money these days.

Mrs. MacDowell has one of the quarters in fairly good condition but she would like to obtain another one — not worn as much.

On the coin, the word "Liberty" is inscribed, along with "In God We Trust" and sculptor MacNeil's R o m a n "M" initial on the right. The other side shows an American Eagle.

But the outstanding charac-

PHOTOMONTAGE BLENDS 1916 AND 1972
. . . Mrs. MacDowell superimposed on Liberty Quarter

Chapter 4

ERRORS

•

FULL HEAD QUARTERS
"THE CONNOISSEUR SECTION"

1929-S. The only known Standing Liberty Quarter that is double struck, obverse and reverse, with another Standing Liberty Quarter. Obviously, the coin is nearly uncirculated. One of a kind and very rare.

Furthest off-center Standing Liberty Quarter known to exist to this date. Extremely rare and has been authenticated by many. A prize piece, sought by many Standing Liberty Quarter enthusiasts. Was thought for many decades, by most of us, to be nonexistent. But! . . .

The above pictured Standing Liberty Quarter is struck out of collar. Not nearly as rare as the pieces pictured above but any error in this series is considered rare and desirable. Like most errors, it, too, is virtually uncirculated. A very interesting piece."

1920-S Struck off-center, with brockage (only on obverse) from the reverse die. The only Standing Liberty Quarter known to exist with brockage.

1928-S Struck out of collar. Off center about 10%. Probably the most "common" Standing Liberty Quarter error, if you can call any Standing Liberty Quarter error "common". Much more available than any other error in the series.

1918-S with incredibility sharp Full Head and shield. Struck off-center about 20%. A good bit more rare than the piece directly above. Coin also has no reeding around the edge. A very beautiful piece.

1919-P: The only known broken planchet that is struck, obverse and reverse. Authenticated by several. The cover coin for the error collector's magazine. Certainly one of your author's pride and joys, and the only coin of it's type known to exist. Rare and most unusual.

One of the most common errors. Slightly off-center and/or slightly out of collar. Have seen a good many of these and they do command a sizable premium. This is the affordable error for most Standing Liberty Quarter enthusiasts.

1927 die trial or set-up coin, testing the striking depth of a new die. Reverse has a very faint outline of the eagle. Obverse has sightly stronger detail. Only one of two known of this rare variety.

Teardrop 1926-S, Contributed by my friends, Aram and Nancy Haroutunian. Extra metal beside Miss Liberty's leg in the shape of a teardrop. To the author's knowledge, the highest grade that has surfaced is an AU coin. Are there higher grades? A very unusual Standing Liberty Quarter cud.

1924 clipped planchet. Anther very unusual, very different Standing Liberty Quarter. As has been said elsewhere, all Standing Liberty Quarter errors are in much demand.

Pictured here is a 1929-S off-center coin, one of the very few your author has seen in his thirty-five years of admiring and collecting Standing Liberty Quarters. All of which carry a fancy price tag. The one pictured was valued at $1,000.00 with another offered at fifty percent off-center at $7,500.00

The above coin shows planchet flaking on the eagle's breast which is very rare in the Standing Liberty Quarter series.

The above photo is courtesy of Rich Schemmer. This coin is the second furthest off-center of the series known to the author at this time. What an immaculate full head.

There are a few love tokens that have been made. Pictured here is an exceptionally mastered one (and a great subject, I might add) though this practice went out of style about the turn of the century. This art was supposed to have been abandoned some 17 years earlier. It makes one wonder why this beautiful work of art was permitted to die. I suppose patience in our society has waned considerably.

Type I	**Type I**	**Type II**
Partial Head	Full Head	Partial Head

Type II	**Type II**	**Type II**
Minimum Full Head	Sharp Full Head	"Ultimate" Full Head

DIAGNOSTICS OF FULL HEAD QUARTERS:

TYPE I — Very distinctly shows all the characteristics of a Full Head Ty. I. (Do not expect any 1916's to be struck this boldly. The worst 1917's are usually better than the best 1916's.) Certainly an immaculate Full Head. Full Head description is a definite line separating Miss Liberty's hair from her temple, her cheekbone, and her throat. On the 1917 Ty. I's frequently the head will be full and raised.

TYPE II — Has a distinct line of separation of the hair from the temple, the cheekbone, and the throat area. Will also have an indentation, or hole, in the hair in the area of the ear. (Hairstyle is modified from Ty. I) The three olive leaves will be complete down to the connecting point and perhaps raised in some very early strikes. (Virtually flattened — especially on most "S" mint marks.) Otherwise, olive leaves will be complete down to Miss Liberty's hairline.

GEM FULL HEAD
STANDING LIBERTY QUARTERS

Taken from *Coin Dealer Newsletter*, Vol. XI, No. 2.

Having spent 40+ years collecting, buying, selling, and attending nearly every major auction that had any appreciable amount of Standing Liberty Quarters, including many West coast auctions, I have purchased or examined as many or more full head Standing Liberty Quarters as any other specialist in the field.

I was looking for full head Standing Liberty Quarters as early as the mid '50's, when BU Standing Liberty Quarters were selling for $5.00 each. I purchased a 1926-D from Kagin's, outright or by auction (I forget which) at the ridiculous sum of $15.00. Many of my friends thought I was foolish. Looked through an uncirculated roll of Sid Smith's in 1954 at the A.N.A. in Cleveland and paid $10.00 for the best one of the roll. Was offered an uncirculated roll, bank wrapped, in 1957—of 1916's for $12,000. Most had full heads. Some sharp. No, I did not buy it. I could not afford it at the time.

I purchased and sold Gene Edwards' personal set. Had permission to advertise them nationwide, but had so many clients for such beautiful specimens that I sold them privately. The most full heads in any of the sets I have ever handled.

Gary Fillers of Chattanooga, Tennessee, had one of the finest sets I have ever seen. Ranked third or fourth. I saw it in 1980 at the Tennessee State show. It sold for mid-six figure money. I examined the set carefully. They were as follows: The 1916—a sharp full head, fully brilliant and as good as or better than the full head MS 65/65 A.N.A.C.S. graded coin that I bought through Silver Towne. All of the 1917 Ty. I's— outstanding MS 67/67's. All of his 1919's—P, D, & S— were "Mind Blowers". 1920-D, 1924-S, 1926-D—all sharp, full heads, MS 67/67. His 1927-S—one of the finest known. Gary refused to break the set for an offer of $25,000 on the 1927-S alone. 1930-P & S—incredible sharp full strikes. Also milky white and frosty.

In and around the A.N.A. in 1980 in Cincinnati, Ohio, I purchased 5 uncirculated sets in all. Many full heads in each set, including (2) 1916's and (2) 1927-S's. One set came from an old friend here in Dayton, Ohio. He was some 20 years putting together this set in the '50's and '60's. This was the most I have ever paid for a single set. WOW!!!

A doctor's group in West Palm Beach owns at least (2) 1916's that yours truly sold them that are full heads. Another doctor in St. Petersburg owns one (A.N.A.C.S. graded) and another doctor in Colorado owns one sold by yours truly. These are only starters and strictly from memory.

In my 40 or so years in numismatics, I have handled several 1916's in the AU 50/55 range with full heads also. "Standing Liberty Quarters" (revised), my 1986 book, on page 101 stated : Value and Rarity: "Price ranks it 5th; quantity ranks it 2nd in scarcity." Have bought and sold nearly 100 pieces over the 40+ years.

I also assisted the Bortin's in their accumulation of Standing Liberty Quarters. I then bought many of the full heads back at their auction in New York.

The number of pieces listed in the following analysis is the number I judge that are still available in today's market. CH BU, MS 65/67, full sharp full head, shield and toes:

1916	The hairstyle for the 1916 is slightly different than on the 1917 Ty.1. The detail from the ear to the crown of her head is slightly lower and the hairlines fall in different directions.
	This accounts for some of the softness of the 1916's. Never have I seen a 1916 with a sharp full head like the 1917. The detail was never put on the die to the same degree. 1916's are characteristically softly struck in the shield as well. Just overall softness altogether. A full strike 1916 could only be compared with another 1916 realistically. Many have the matte proof effect; also light, medium or heavy russet toning. I judge 25-30 pieces exist on today 's market (and they're going to be softly struck).
1917 Ty.I	Most minted were full head. Many MS 65 and MS 67's. At least 2-3,000 pieces still exist.
1917-D Ty.I	Maybe nearly as many as Ty.I "P" mint, but most probably less. As few as 1,000-1,200 pieces exist because it is a branch mint.
1917-S Ty.I	Much rarer than the "D" mint. Many soft strikes, but still 600+ pieces on today's market.
1917 Ty.II	Many times fewer than Ty.I: Wonder coins do exist of this date. Many beautiful light blue toned coins exist of this date, 1,000 pieces or so.
1917-D Ty.II	Quality begins to deteriorate on this series (also a branch mint). 150-300 pieces in existence today?
1917-S Ty.II	About on the same par. But would only estimate 100-125 still exist
1918	Many more exist of this date than you may think. I owned an original roll of these, with 15 pieces full head and bought and sold about another 50 pieces over the years. Would give this date 500 or more pieces.
1918-D	One of the little known scarce Standing Liberty Quarters. Usually flat from the knee to waist, although with full heads. Have owned or sold at least 25 pieces. I would give it 60-100 pieces.

1918/17-S   It is in print by another author as "unknown". (Editor of The Coin Dealer Newsletter reported seeing a photo of one that did exist when this article ran in February, 1986). I bought one in Auction '80, Lot #1252 in Cincinnati. Mailed it to a collector in New York and the good old Post Office lost it. Bought one from a Chicago dealer in AU. But it had a full head and made a collector in Michigan very happy. (He had been looking for one for 15 years, before he met me). A West coast dealer had one in Atlanta at the A.N.A. for $15,000. Coin had a full head, but softly struck in the torso, but was a full MS 65 otherwise. The previously mentioned photographed coin resides in the state of Florida. Sharp full head. Head and shoulders above any other piece I have ever seen. Probably 5 pieces or less exist of this date and I would value this one at $100,000.

1918-S   More available than the "D" but very tough to find in full head, MS 65-67. About 25 pieces or so have been bought and sold by yours truly. 15-25 pieces currently available.

1919   Many outstanding coins of this date. Common, if any date can be called common. Second only to the 1917 Ty.I in the pre'25 era. Maybe as high as 500 pieces available.

1919-D   A few wonder coins exist of this date. Thought I owned the finest until A.N.A. Atlanta, 1977. Bought one on the floor. Paid double "bid". Sold it to a Brooklyn, New York collector. Much rarer than the 1919-S. I have bought and sold 10-15 pieces. Today's market would give it a 20-30 piece rating.

1919-S   A bit more common than the "D", but certainly not much. Usually mushy or soft, even when full head. A few outstanding pieces exist even in today's market. 15-25 pieces probably available today.

1920   The third most common pre-'25. Lots of full heads. Maybe as many as 400? Have handled as many as 100 or more over the last 40 years. About three coins in 100 that are described as full heads in ads and catalogs meet that criteria. A close second to the 1919. About 300-400 pieces.

1920-D   Much more common than its counterpart, the "S". Maybe as many as 25-30 pieces are available in today's market. Most advertised as such are not. Seems to come in MS 63 full head many times more frequently than in MS 65 full head.

1920-S   Much rarer than present wholesale or retail prices indicate. A very much sought after coin in MS65 FH grade. Missing from most such sets. A Chicago collector and I looked for five years before we found a true MS 65 full head, shield, toes, etc. etc. Probably less than 20 pieces available today, all MS grades considered.

1921   Some real "mind blowers" exist of this coin. Wire rim. Full head. Needle sharp shield - vertical and horizontal. Deep strikes. I have probably handled as many as 25 or so in my 40 years as a numismatist. Since the advent of encapsulation, this date has been proven to be a bit tougher than the 1923-S (but not much). Maybe as many as 30-40 pieces of this date exist today.

1923 Many outstanding examples of this one exist also; many of which come frosty or creamy white. Have handled as many as 25 or more of this date, also. Years ago (prior to the '80's) there were many around, but very few were looking for the ultimate. Auction '83 contained a roll described as follows: "Roll of 40 coins. Mint State 65 to 67. A lovely original roll of Standing Liberty Quarters. Each frosty brilliant uncirculated specimen displays full blazing mint lustre. One of the few original Brilliant Uncirculated rolls still in existence and should be carefully examined as it contains many full head specimens. Sold as one lot of 40 coins." (Lot #1702). Fetched $23,000. Said to contain many full heads - and did. I rate the availability of this one at 100-125 pieces. Sharp full heads are tough all the way down to AU - sold a CH <u>AU</u> FH for as much as $350.00.

1923-S Seems to be not as tough as the 1921, though mintage is 1.916 vs 1.360 million. Have handled 25-35 pieces that fall into the "almost - but no cigar" category (which would satisfy most). Have purchased some over the years from other dealers. Rate this one at 30-50 pieces.

1924 A reasonable number of these exist in MS 65 full head, and it is thought to be a bit scarcer than the 1920. Many coins of this date come in a gun metal blue, with some pieces having a granular surface also. Very attractive coin to those of us who appreciate a toned coin. More in the 150-250 piece range.

1924-D This date frequently will have full head, shield, and toes and yet have the top half or third of the date missing. Have examined many examples of the progressive die break through the top half of the date. The explanation for this is that the die eventually broke away completely. If you include the MS 65 full head pieces with 1/2 or 2/3 of the date, you would have several hundred pieces. If you say it must have full date, then probably 100 pieces, give or take a few. Very scarce.

1924-S Scarcer than the 1924-D. Usually much stronger at the date. Have purchased and sold perhaps 15-20 pieces in my years as a professional numismatist. Would put the availability at 75-80 pieces , more or less.

1925 A goodly amount exist of this date. Many of them full head. However, they are softly struck on the shield - vertical and horizontal lines. One of the toughest "P" mints to find if you are looking for a full head, shield, toes, etc. Frequently comes very brilliant. Maybe in the 200-250 range.

1926 Recessed date can usually be located without a great deal of difficulty. Many have razor sharp olive leaves and separation from temple of Miss Liberty; some even have raised leaves. But, these are few and far between. Have handled 20 or so of such caliber. Would rate this date about 100-125 pieces available today.

1926-D The classic flat head. True MS 65 full heads are very rare and even at "Trends" price of $30,000, it is still much underpriced. Have bought or sold 15 pieces or so in all grades of MS. I've seen frosty white full heads, and some that looked polished. (Think these were the first few pieces struck after a die had just been retooled and polished). A doctor's group in Florida owns three pieces. A collector in Florida owns two and three other pieces reside elsewhere. For a full head MS 65, would rate this coin much rarer than the 1916. Probably 15-25 pieces or less? I know there is one in Colorado that is still raw and would fit the MS 65 FH/MS 66 FH category.

1926-S Extremely rare. Have handled only 10-12 pieces of this date. A very close second to the 1927-S. Does come flashy, with lots of eye appeal MS 65, but only 60-80% head and then the rest of the coin will be struck up to standard. Would rate this date and mintmark at a dozen or less pieces in today's market.

1927 Seem to be many of this date on today's market in last 3-4 years. Have seen maybe as many as the 1930-P. Would give it 100-150. Fairly "common" if you could call a full head Standing Liberty Quarter common. This date frequently comes very brilliant.

1927-D Much more available than the 1926-D. More likely than not, the head will lack some fine detail. Very tough in super full head. Would give it a 125-150, but there are some available if you look hard.

1927-S Very, very tough! Have handled less than 10 pieces in sharp full head MS 65. At this writing, only one MS 65 FH and one MS 66 FH appear in the reports. AU full head seems to be two to three times more available than uncirculated pieces. Most advertised '27-S raw full heads are not!! Probably a 10 piece or less availability. TOUGH!!!

1928 A close second to the 1927, though realistically a bit tougher. This date also comes very brilliant, and with lots of eye appeal. 75-100 available.

1928-D Very scarce. Closely priced in relation to the 1929-D and should be slightly scarcer. This date and mintmark should be seven times or greater than the 1928-P. 30-50 pieces on today's market.

1928-S This date and mintmark can come with a lot of brilliance and also many frosty or creamy white pieces. Outstanding in many ways, but - only 70-80% head. Usually, very weak at the temple. Would rate this date and mintmark in the 150-200 range on today's market.

THE OVER-MINTMARKS:

1928-D/D Always accompanied by the die break on the obverse that starts at the last star on the right at MacNeil's initials; continues across the pedestal (just under her foot) all the way across the date into the last star on the left. Also some continue through the "D" - either half way up the "D" or through the bottom fold in her gown to the second star on left. Just under the hem of her gown, a very light pimple of metal appears.

1928-S/s Discovered about 25 years ago by yours truly. Consequently, many pieces went the circulated route and very few gems in MS 65-67 FH exist. Usually sought out by the connoisseur who wants one of every variety. Easily seen with low magnification. The lower serif of the "S" protrudes from under the top "S". Very, very tough in high uncirculated grades.

The bottom one-third of the "S" beneath the lower part of the serif is easily visible with 10X magnification. Die break from Miss Liberty's first three toes over to the top of the "1" of the date.

1928-D/S About as tough as its sister the 1928-S/s. Very few in the MS 65-67 FH range. The grading services do not recognize this on the holders at this writing, but hopefully the numbering system and diagnostics will change that. Again, easily seen with low (10X) magnification. Probably just one die used for obverse. The top serif of the "S" is usually very distinct. A crossbar through the middle of the "D"; the bottom serif of "S" mintmark is protruding from beneath the "D" which usually puts a tail on the bottom portion of the "D".

1928-S/D   Probably the hardest to detect. The "D" is just a blob under low magnification - all you can see is a tail on the "D" and top and bottom of the "D". Occasionally this has a die break - resembling the one on the D/D, but usually higher on the left gown fold. Look carefully before you buy, since the third party grading services are very reluctant to encapsulate these varieties. A.N.A.C.S. does slab the D/D only at this point in time. Most likely one die used here as well.

Rarity is about the same for the overmint-marks: 1928-D/S, S/D and S/S. Prices run about 2-3 times the regular price as all are very difficult to come by in Full Head and high grade. The die is weakened when another strike is given to the die to establish this rarity.

1929   Many full heads of this date are available on today's market. Many are nice. Another year for frosty BU coins, with a bit of searching. Maybe as many as 600-1,000 of this date. All "P" mints from 1926-'30 are out there today. Have personally bought and sold 300 or more over a 40 year span.

1929-D   Looked at by many as a "common" date, but not so. Very underrated coin in the series. Usual weakness in head and inner shield. A lot of "almost" (about 90-95X head) coins of this date and mintmark. Takes a lot of looking. Would rate this date 25-50 on today's market. Many have the gun metal toning; very attractive. Full head, shield and toes. Rates very close to the 1916 in scarcity.

1929-S   Have handled 25-35 pieces of this date and mintmark over the years. The hoard that surfaced in 1975 in California had about 50 pieces. Bought and sold some 15-20 at that time. This date frequently comes fully brilliant or with "full mint bloom", although not all of those have full head, and are MS 65-67. Many frosty pieces here, also. Would give this one about 200-300.

1930   The most "common" full head, shield and toes of the entire series, if you can indeed call any full head Standing Liberty Quarter common. But The C.D.N. and other numismatic publications still rate it with the 1930-S (and other dates) when there should be a marked difference. You can find at least 10 to 1 of this date compared to the 1930-S. Would put this date at 500-650 pieces.

1930-S   It is in print by another author - "never found with a full head," but.... there are many full heads of this date and mintmark. The price should be 3-5 times greater than its sister date, 1930-P. Have handled 100+ pieces that are frosty-white or creamy-white Gem full heads, and of course they bring considerably above the "Greysheet" price. Two such pieces reside in the state of Florida. Would rate this one at 200-250 pieces on today's market.

Please keep in mind that when this article originally appeared in February of 1986, third-party grading was in its infancy and many figures used at that time are now incorrect. We have made an extensive effort to update those figures, and 10 more years of experience. If you have any questions concerning these, please feel free to call us and we can (hopefully) help you out.

Keep in mind as you read "bought" and "sold" in this article, I was buying and selling Standing Liberty Quarters when I knew of no one else who was. I did not advertise until the late 1950's or early 1960's, so it was done by word of mouth. I was looking for full heads when I knew only one or two others who had any concern for a full head. I heard many times: "They all look alike to me." One collector mistook full head to mean the circle on the head next to the rim to have a full and separated line from the field and rim. Awareness has certainly increased over the years!

Chapter 5

YEAR & MINTMARK ANALYSIS

I would like very much to go on record concerning the 1916/1917 Ty.I's. Calling them both Type I is an atrocity with complete disregard for the difference in the head design of the two pieces. Perhaps 1916 Ty.I-A and 1917 Ty.I-B would be appropriate. Firstly, the sash that Miss Liberty holds across her body is incused on the 1916 and raised on the 1917 Ty.I. The hairstyle on the 1916 slightly overlaps onto her forehead, but does not on the 1917 Ty.I. The 1917 Ty.I has several locks of hair down her forehead and to the ear. The 1916 has straighter hair lines with a single lock above the ear that determines whether it is or is not a Full Head on the 1916. 1916's are weakly struck and 1917 Ty.I's are the strongest strikes of the whole series. On the 1916 rivets in shield are weak; 1917 Ty.I rivets are strong.

I would like very much to see the grading services add to the Full Head minimum requirement description, "Sharp Full Head" and "Ultimate Full Head", very much like the "PL" and "DMPL" on the dollar series. This might be a bit confusing at first, but would help in the long run to clear up some of the Full Head confusion.

Please keep in mind, as you read this book, that certification by a third party grading service does not eliminate market risk, nor does it guarantee associated risks regarding grading. Past performance can in no way be used to "predict" future value.

When referring to the published statistics in the "PCGS Population Report" and the "NGC Census Report" we would like to remind you that these figures are in some instances inaccurate due to resubmissions of coins for a higher grade. When the coin is broken out of a holder for resubmission to the grading service, if the insert is not returned to them, the coin continues to appear in the reports. i.e.: if there are 5 items listed for a certain date/mintmark in MS65 FH and one of them is broken out (but the insert is retained by customer) when the coin is slabbed MS65 FH again 6 pieces would appear in the column, but only 5 would exist. Each time the item is tried for a higher grade and grades the same, the number inflates, so the item could appear in both reports, yet only one item exists.

All population report data are based on March 1996 PCGS Population and NGC Census reports.

1916

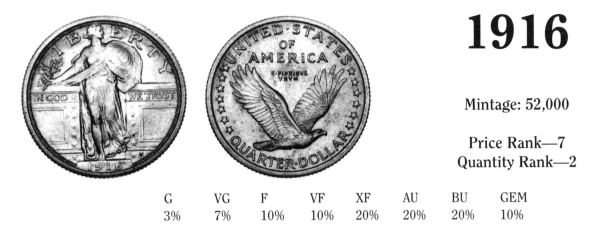

Mintage: 52,000

Price Rank—7
Quantity Rank—2

G	VG	F	VF	XF	AU	BU	GEM
3%	7%	10%	10%	20%	20%	20%	10%

3% OR LESS STRUCK WITH FULL HEADS

This coin has long been the most sought-after coin in the series, usually more than the 1918/7-S.
The 1916 has, of course, the lowest mintage of all dates and mintmarks, except the overdate. There are some 1917, Ty. I's that have been altered to 1916. By using at least a ten power magnifier, it is usually easy to detect. There are several ways to tell a 1916 dateless coin.

#1: On the high grades, the gown drapes below the edge of the ship's sideboards.

#2: The gown folds are different along Miss Liberty's leg. (Does not touch leg.)

#3: Her gown is incused instead of raised, as on the 1917 and later coins (in the right hand area).

#4: (The one yours truly likes best of all) The reed above Miss Liberty's head is cut in half to make room for her head. I like this one best, as you can tell in very low grades.

#5: Miss Liberty's great toe slightly overlaps the base and, facing the coin, Miss Liberty's gown touches the left side of her foot and is not as curved at the bottom as the 1917 Ty. I or any other date. On the altered date, her gown does indeed touch the foot, and the bottom edge of the gown is much more rounded.

#6: Fingers are "mushed" together on 1916; small and separated on the 1917 Ty. 1.

There were many 1916 and 1917, Ty. I's that were struck from rusty dies that gave them a satin-looking finish at first glance, but they are not to be confused with the very rare matte proof of the same year.
The hair detail is different in style than the 1917 Ty. l. Top of head: last 3 curls seem to fall toward back of head.
Hair detail is almost incused-most always very softly struck or "mushy" as some prefer to call it.

GRADING:

The 1916 is always softly struck in the head and shield. The dies were completed in July, 1916 and set until December 16 before any striking took place. Rust knocked off all high points or they.were polished off in removing the rust. Striking dies are made of high speed steel, and it is difficult to rustproof them.

OBVERSE

Due consideration should be given in grading Uncirculated 1916's. Weak horizontal and vertical shield lines. Head is weak in ear, neck, throat. Line separating hair is not distinct. Also, rivets on center shield are usually missing on many, even mint state coins.

REVERSE

Reverse is frequently strong. Full feathers on eagle's body and head. Sometimes even a wire rim. Just a LITTLE wear makes this date look like an XF or VF coin because of the weakness in the strike.

* * *

AVAILABILITY OF FULL HEADS:

		MS65	MS66	MS67
FULL HEADS:	PCGS	16	2	2
	NGC	1	3	0
NON-FULL HEADS:	PCGS	14	3	0
	NGC	17	4	0

The 1916 Standing Liberty Quarter is probably the most sought-after piece in the entire series, mostly because it is the first year of issue, and then due to its low mintage: 52,000 pieces. This makes it the second lowest mintage of the series, with the 1918/7-S the lowest at an estimated mintage of 15,000? pieces. The current population at P.C.G.S. of MS 65 FH pieces is 16, with a strong possibility that 1/3-1/2 of those have been resubmitted. I must confess that all of my research into the P.C.G.S. Population Report and the N.G.C. Census Report shows that the figures are off by at least 10-15% due to many dealers (including yours truly) breaking out encapsulated coins in the early years and not returning the inserts. The grading service began to allow 50 cents for each insert returned to them and that did stimulate many of the dealers to return them from that point onward. The inserts were then processed by the grading services and removed from their respective reports. I have, however, personally witnessed many Standing Liberty Quarters being broken out at the coin shows, and the inserts thrown away. Thus, the reports are not accurate despite the grading services' efforts to make them so. The reports are inflated on some dates (perhaps by as much as 50% in some cases) and particularly on the dates that "Trends" for 2-3 times more from MS 64 FH to MS 65 FH. The 1918-S MS 64 FH comes to mind. It is about $7,000 in MS 64 FH, but moves up to $23/25,000 in MS 65 FH.

Just prior to the Anaheim, California A.N.A. in August, 1995 there were 4 MS 66 FH 1916's on the reports. Then, suddenly they reflected 2 pieces in MS 66 FH and 2 pieces in MS 67 FH, with both pieces appearing in one dealer's case at that convention. The greater the money difference between the grades, the greater is the possibility someone will break them out of the existing holder and resubmit for the higher grade and higher dollar. It would be great if all inserts were kept and returned to the services when a break-out occurs.

At this writing, both MS 67 FH P.C.G.S. graded 1916's are looking for new homes. One of the MS 66 FH's lives in Florida; the other lives out west. I placed the one in Florida and am aware of the whereabouts of the other piece. The three N.G.C. pieces* are also accounted for with one piece on the market at this time (graded within the last 5 months) and the other is in strong hands in Florida.

*Since NGC encapsulated the third piece - which is on the market at this time - the second piece has found a new home in the mid-west.

Matte Proof
1917
Type I

Walter H. Breen

Box 352, Berkeley, CA 94701

Cincinnati ANA
July 23, 1988

TO WHOM IT MAY CONCERN

This certifies that I have examined the accompanying coin and that I unhesitatingly declare it a genuine 1917 Type I quarter proof (matte variant).

On comparing it to another such proof I find that the striking quality is the same, showing far more detail on head, shield, central drapery, feet, breast feathers, &c., than do the regularly seen full head 1917's; the surfaces, obviously untampered, differ from those of business strikes.

Number surviving is uncertain. Within the last 20-odd years I have seen possibly 7 specimens.

Respectfully submitted
Walter Breen

1917
Type I

Mintage: 8,740,000

Price Rank—31
Quantity Rank—27

G	VG	F	VF	XF	AU	BU	GEM
5%	5%	5%	10%	10%	40%	15%	10%

80% STRUCK WITH FULL HEADS

This date and mintmark is probably the best overall strike of the entire series and the most available with full heads in a direct ratio with the number minted of any other year.

This date usually comes very well struck. It is also the coin most used for the Type I Standing Liberty Quarter in Type Sets. Common as it is, the demand is great and a Full Head still commands a $900-1,500 premium and up.

The first coin your author bought with a Full Head-he paid the ridiculous price of $7.50 for it and thought he had overpaid because other Standing Liberty Quarters were selling for $5.00. (I still own that coin.)

This date and mintmark is the classic strong strike. At the same time, do not grade other dates by these standards. If you compare this coin with most other dates of the series, you would not buy the other dates. No need to relax any grading standards on this one.

In 1984, about 200-300 of these coins surfaced in Indiana that had been cast. Not only were they a poor job, but the clapboards on the side of the ship (on either side of Miss Liberty) had been ground in as though by a fine surface grinder. Lines were too perfect. Coin World ran a fine, informative article on it.

GRADING:

OBVERSE

The classic full strike. All details are sharp. It is not fair by any stretch of the imagination to compare any other date or mintmark with this date. Head is almost always full, even on many AU's (some XF's). All lines, vertical and horizontal are usually complete. Also, all ten toes are usually struck up. Frequently, a wire rim.

REVERSE

Is most always full in every detail. All feathers on eagle's breast distinct. Forward edge of eagle's wings is struck up fully.

* * *

AVAILABILITY OF FULL HEADS:

		MS65	MS66	MS67
FULL HEADS:	PCGS	327	74	8
	NGC	105	33	2
NON-FULL HEADS:	PCGS	252	29	0
	NGC	221	36	3

The eight pieces of this date and mintmark are second in population only to the 1930 MS67 FH at P.C.G.S. I have placed most of these, but did not handle a couple of them, as I did not agree that they should be graded MS67 FH. Usually flashy white, with just a hint of light golden, these are much sought after by type collectors, as no higher grade exists in this date. A very interesting side note: N.G.C. has graded three MS67 non-full heads and P.C.G.S. has graded zero MS67 non-full heads. These three N.G.C. pieces may be left from the old days when N.G.C. assumed all 1917 Type I's were full head and did not place the designation on Type I holders. If these three pieces have not been sent back through for inclusion of the "Full Head" designation, then three more full head pieces exist in the MS67 Type I column. As you can see, in the P.C.G.S. and N.G.C. publications, they have a combined population of sixty-five of non-full head pieces grading MS66, proving you cannot assume anything. You are usually surprised by it happening.

1917-D
Type I

Mintage: 1,509,200

Price Rank—26
Quantity Rank—7

G	VG	F	VF	XF	AU	BU	GEM
10%	10%	15%	15%	15%	10%	10%	15%

25% STRUCK WITH FULL HEADS

The 1917-D, Type I Standing Liberty Quarters are generally available, as most first-year coins are usually saved in abundance. (This was the first year the public saw the coins as the 1916 was not placed into circulation until January 17, 1917.) As always, lots of new dies were standing by for use in striking the new coins. Being struck at a branch mint, the 1917-D, Type I was not struck as well as the coins that were struck this year at the Philadelphia mint.

There are large and small mintmarks of this date which, of course, comes from the fact that each worker who installs the dies had his own set of tools where he put on the mint mark. There are about three variations of sizes in these mint marks.

The 1917-D, Type I only sells for about two times the price of the 1917-P, Type I; but in reality, the coin is at least 3 to 5 times more rare (or even greater). Would look at this coin for long term.

This mintmark is about in the middle of the road as far as grading is concerned. You should expect most features to be struck up, but sometimes a weak point or two, such as rivets on the shield or weak spots on the stars will be detected. There are some soft strikes of this date and mint mark-usually in the head and shield. Hair between ear and top of head is not bold (no separation of temple and hairline). Usually fully lustrous. Frequently comes with a strange frosty appearance, but under close scrutiny (5-10 x) chalky surface looks as though it has been coated with a white substance; probably not done at the mint.

GRADING:

OBVERSE

Some concessions in grading should be made, but not as much as the 1917-S, Type I. Very much like its sister date,1917-P. This date comes very strong. A full, sharp head, shield and toes. Not quite as nice as the "P" mint, but a very close 2nd. Excellent branch mint strike. Frequently comes creamy white as well as frosty with a cartwheel effect.

REVERSE

Usually medium to strong strike. Many breast feathers are here that are missing from most Standing Liberty Quarters.

* * *

AVAILABILITY OF FULL HEADS:

		MS65	MS66	MS67
FULL HEADS:	PCGS	97	30	1
	NGC	37	8	1
NON-FULL HEADS:				
	PCGS	71	10	1
	NGC	67	9	1

This date and mintmark seems to be adequate for the collector demand in MS66 FH, but many are still looking for the elusive grade of MS67 FH. At this writing, none have been slabbed in MS68. I have seen both MS67 FH's but did not care for one of them and consequently did not choose to handle it. The second piece is exceptionally nice and a full MS67. Many of the slabbed pieces from both P.C.G.S. and N.G.C. are very colorful and those who are looking for the blast white piece or the light golden piece are still looking. There are very few of these MS66 FH pieces with which I disagree. As with most Type I pieces, the head is almost always Full and sharp, but this statement deteriorates with the three mintmarks: P is best; D is less: S is much less (when compared to the "P" mint). All, however, look strong if compared to the 1916 - which is a type all by itself and should not be "lumped" in with the Type I pieces.

1917-S
Type I

Mintage: 1,952,000

Price Rank—22
Quantity Rank—15

G	VG	F	VF	XF	AU	BU	GEM
20%	10%	10%	10%	10%	20%	10%	10%

5% STRUCK WITH FULL HEADS

Since the mintage of 1917-S, Type I is some 443,000 more than the 1917-D, Type I, it would lead one to think they are worth less. However, being the magic "S" mintmark, the facilities leave a lot to be desired. The 1917-S, Type I is by far the toughest of the three to locate with a full head. As is usually the case of Standing Liberty Quarters, the more that are minted, the more soft strikes and the more flat heads there are on a ratio basis. A much underrated coin on today's market. It is probably 3 to 5 times more rare than the 1917-D, Type I, as it is usually unfairly compared to the 1917, Type I (and priced accordingly). Not so. It is much rarer.

GRADING:

OBVERSE

Since most were struck rather softly, this date and mintmark is the weakest of all 1917 Type I's. Frequently, the first digit of the date is very weak; even the entire date is occasionally weak. Relax to some degree on the normal grading of the Type I's. Weak rivets on shield (especially #2 and #3)* head flat or softly struck, though much eye appeal. Even an Uncirculated coin could easily be called XF or AU. Know who you buy from and get a receipt describing the coin in full.

REVERSE

The same is true of the reverse as it is of the obverse. Coin is weakly struck (the weakest of all 1917 Ty. I's). Very weak especially in the breast feathers as well as eagle's head and tail feathers.

*Author's note: keep this in mind when buying XF and AU. A little wear on a weakly struck coin will appear greater than it is in reality.

* * *

* When referring to rivets your author numbers the bottom rivet as #1 (close to Miss Liberty's body). Then continuing clockwise: #2, #3, etc.

AVAILABILITY OF FULL HEADS:

		MS65	MS66	MS67
FULL HEADS:	PCGS	46	14	0
	NGC	8	8	1
NON-FULL HEADS:				
	PCGS	38	9	1
	NGC	27	12	1

I strongly suspect this is one of those dates and mintmarks in which many have been broken out and resubmitted. The population publications seem to reflect a bit higher numbers than availability exhibits. P.C.G.S. shows forty-six pieces of MS65; only fourteen pieces of MS66; and NO MS67 Full Heads. The reported MS67 FH Philadelphia and Denver pieces prove the statement made earlier in this analysis - the San Francisco Mint is much weaker then the other two mints. N.G.C. has eight pieces of MS65 listed; eight MS66, and one MS67 Full Head. This is an extremely rare coin in MS67 FH. The low number of N.G.C. pieces, again may be due to the fact that they did not place "Full Head" designation on Type I quarters in the early days of encapsulation. All Type I quarters were assumed to be full head by N.G.C. at that time. The figures would be changed if the older pieces were sent back to N.G.C. for the designation.

1917
Type II

Mintage: 13,880,000

Price Rank—32
Quantity Rank—36

G	VG	F	VF	XF	AU	BU	GEM
5%	5%	10%	10%	20%	10%	20%	20%

10% STRUCK WITH FULL HEADS

Note the modification of the hair-do, eagle, stars and chain mail vest that was added. This created stress on the obverse die to produce the raised hair around Miss Standing Liberty's head, and caused the entire obverse to be weakly struck. This, in part, accounts for so many weak strikes. There are also less rivets on the shield and broader reeds and beads on the rim than the Type I. Full Heads of this date are in the more common category than other dates with about 10% struck with Full Heads. Many coins of this date do come frosty and are more desirable to those who appreciate this lovely appearance. As with all dates with a high mintage, do not be misled that they are "common". No standing Liberty Quarter in Full Head is common. They are all scarce. These are just easier to locate than some other dates. When the term "more common" is used, it is meant comparatively speaking!!! This is the best strike of the 1917, Ty. II, P-D-S, but not as strong a strike as the Type I Philadelphia mint.

GRADING:

OBVERSE

You can expect normal grading standards to apply to this date and mintmark. Frequently, this coin will have a Full Head, but not be an M.S. 65/65 coin. Have seen as low a grade as AU that has a Full Head and sometimes even XF.

REVERSE

Normal grading is the rule of the day on this date and mintmark on the reverse as well as the obverse. Generally speaking, the reverse of the Type II was stronger struck than the obverse. Expect feathers to be strong, both in wings and the breast area. Tail feathers are usually a strong point, too.

* * *

AVAILABILITY OF FULL HEADS:

		MS65	MS66	MS67
FULL HEADS:	PCGS	105	19	0
	NGC	56	14	0
NON-FULL HEADS:				
	PCGS	50	13	0
	NGC	26	6	0

This date and mintmark seems to be plentiful in MS65 and MS66 FH's, but very elusive in the MS67 FH grade, missing from both major services. In my 1976 book, I made a statement that some dates and mintmarks were just never struck up to perfection (meaning today's MS67 and up). You would normally expect this date and mintmark to be plentiful in all grades.

I have found homes for many of the MS66 FH's and they were all nice and mostly white to light golden. Amazing as it may seem, they looked so much alike that they seemed to be struck simultaneously and all from the same type of blank planchet.

1917-D
Type II

Mintage: 6,224;400

Price Rank—17
Quantity Rank—23

G	VG	F	VF	XF	AU	BU	GEM
10%	10%	15%	15%	10%	20%	10%	10%

5% STRUCK WITH FULL HEADS

This coin has a mintage of less than half of its counterpart, the 1917, Type II, yet its price today is 4 to 5 times greater. Your author thinks it, too, is one of the sleepers of the Standing Liberty Quarters. Most branch mints are commonly weakly struck, and this date is no exception. Full Heads are more available than previously stated, but still worth at least 4 times more than non-FH. (Since my book was first issued in 1976, I have continued to find this to be a very elusive date in Full Head, M.S. 65/67.) Very seldom available at today's prices.

GRADING:

OBVERSE

Again, use the middle of the road grading. Most features are moderately well struck, with some concessions to be made: weak inner shield, but strong date and folds in gown, or vice versa. Somewhat paralleled to the 1924-D in that the top half of the date is frequently missing, though the rest of the coin is fully struck. This also happens (though a little less frequently) in the 1918-D.

REVERSE

Eagle's breast feathers and pin feathers are a bit stronger on Uncirculated coins. These highest spots go quickly.

* * *

This 1917-D Type II is one of those coins with re-engraved hair around Miss Liberty's head as well as the three olive leaves. Note the olive leaves are not the right style, nor is the hairstyle as it should be. This piece also has re-engraved toes.

AVAILABILITY OF FULL HEADS:

		MS65	MS66	MS67
FULL HEADS:	PCGS	22	2	0
	NGC	12	1	0
NON-FULL HEADS:				
	PCGS	19	6	0
	NGC	15	7	0

The placing of all MS65 and MS66 FH pieces from both major grading services would not be difficult on this Type 2 piece. I did place the N.G.C. piece and many of the MS65 FH pieces from both services, but none of the P.C.G.S. MS66 FH. The MS66 FH appeared in the May 27-29, 1990 Father Flanagan's Boys Home Sale by Superior Galleries as Lot #3723 and brought $12,000.00 plus the buyer's premium. It then appeared in the Harold Rothenberger Collection sale by Superior Auction Galleries on January 31 - February 1, 1994 as Lot #1350 and brought $8,500.00 plus the buyer's premium. It now resides in the western portion of our country.

Normally, when this date and mintmark has a Full Head it is nice and full; however a few are in MS65 FH holders that I do not think should be in those holders. This occurs in both services.

Before the softness of the coin market, this coin was fetching $10-12,000 in MS65 FH. This was also when only 2 or 3 pieces had surfaced in the population publications. I feel that many of these have been broken out for resubmission and the population is way off in MS64 FH (hoping for a MS65 FH grade) and MS65 FH (hoping for an MS66 or even 67 FH grade).

The grading services have been much more exacting in overall condition of the coin and are taking a long, hard look at the hairline before calling it a Full Head, yet there are still some recent encapsulations with which I do not agree with the grade. Just for the record, if I do not agree with the grade on the holder, I do not handle the coin. My advice to anyone: if you do not agree with the grade on the plastic - do not buy it. Buy the coin and not the holder.

1917-S
Type II

Mintage: 5,552,000

Price Rank—20
Quantity Rank—21

G	VG	F	VF	XF	AU	BU	GEM
5%	10%	25%	25%	10%	10%	10%	5%

3% LESS STRUCK WITH FULL HEADS

A common mistake is to compare the 1917-S, Type II with the 1917-D, Type II because of its mintage figures. This would indicate only a slight bit more in price than the Denver mint — but this is not so. It is probably 3 to 5 times more scarce in Full Heads than the Denver mint, and probably 5 to 10 times more rare than the Philadelphia mint of 1917, Type II. It is one of the softest strikes of the 1917's, both Type I and Type II. Full heads <u>are</u> scarce in today's numismatic market.

GRADING:

OBVERSE

In grading circulated coins of this date, some "give and take" in certain areas should be exercised, as most were struck with flat heads. Very little circulation drops the grade to extra fine or even very fine. Many flat heads of this date grade a sharp M.S. 65, except hair detail from forehead to ear. Weakest of all 1917 Type I's or II. Price is paralleled with the rest of the 1917's, but should not be. Usually no inner shield lines, vertical or horizontal or incomplete. Chain mail is sometimes softly struck or "mushy" as well as the rivets on the shield. Most usually the #3 and #4 rivets are flat or missing altogether.

REVERSE

Usually above average strike. Should meet normal grading criteria. Weakly struck Unc. could be called XF or AU. Again, know your dealer and get a receipt.

* * *

#C-5095. A major die break on a 1917-S Ty II. Probably completely chipped out on next strike.

AVAILABILITY OF FULL HEADS:

		MS65	MS66	MS67
FULL HEADS:	PCGS	29	4	2
	NGC	7	1	0
NON-FULL HEADS:				
	PCGS	38	8	0
	NGC	25	2	0

The "S" Type 2 is extremely rare in MS66 FH and in MS67 FH. Only 2 pieces have been slabbed MS67 FH and only at P.C.G.S. This could be because P.C.G.S. has been in the grading service business longer than N.G.C., or it could be because approximately 1/10 of the U.S. population lives in the state of California, making P.C.G.S. more popular in California. Also, all "S" mints are characteristically weaker. The N.G.C. piece and 2 of the 4 P.C.G.S. 66 FH pieces were placed through our offices - all were nice MS66 FH pieces, although the N.G.C. piece was a bit more toned, but all there with a sharp Full Head.

1918

Mintage: 14,240,000

Price Rank—27
Quantity Rank—37

G	VG	F	VF	XF	AU	BU	GEM
10%	15%	15%	20%	15%	10%	5%	10%

5% STRUCK WITH FULL HEADS

The 1918 is one of the better struck coins overall, and the strongest strike up to this point, (not including the 1917 Ty. 1). On many, the top half of the date is weakly struck. It is there, but soft. The 1918 is not as strongly struck as the 1917 and the 1919. Full Head specimens are much scarcer than today's prices indicate. Pictured, is a superb Gem, and was probably the first piece struck from new dies. This is the closest to a Prooflike your author has ever seen. Not only a Full Head, but on this piece you can see the separation of the cheek bone and the separation of the hair on her head from the front curl to the back of Miss Liberty's head. Outstanding coin in every respect.

This date and mintmark does come nice with a bit of perseverance. Keep looking!! Seems to have a much deeper rim than other dates, and does come superbly struck. (Not all 1918's fit this category, or course.)

GRADING:

As with most Philadelphia strikes, all grades should be expected to come up to normal grading standards.

OBVERSE
First digit or two of date are frequently weak. Shield is usually strong.

REVERSE
Usually, there, but weak. Again, may be a true AU, but wear on feather says "XF or less." Some XF and AU coins of this date still have Full Heads also.

* * *

AVAILABILITY OF FULL HEADS:

#C-5105. Currently slabbed by ANACS as 1918/1918. It is much clearer in person than this picture shows.

		MS65	MS66	MS67
FULL HEADS:	PCGS	30	10	0
	NGC	19	9	1
NON-FULL HEADS:				
	PCGS	44	7	0
	NGC	25	8	0

This "common" date should be available in abundance, but the limited number of pieces that are in holders does not bear out this assumption. Quite the contrary. I placed the only N.G.C. MS67 FH and it has light golden toning with an outstanding head! It is a little colorful, but an immaculate full head piece. Sharp, sharp! None has graded MS67 FH at P.C.G.S., nor has P.C.G.S. graded a non-full head MS67 at this writing. Probably the "sleeper" of the "P" mints in the entire series in higher grades - MS66 FH and up.

1918-D

Mintage: 7,380,000

Price Rank—15
Quantity Rank—26

G	VG	F	VF	XF	AU	BU	GEM
10%	15%	20%	20%	15%	10%	5%	5%

3% STRUCK WITH FULL HEADS

Having examined many 1918-D's, there are many that have good strikes, but most fall into average or poor strikes. This is one of the most underrated coins in the series and seldom comes with a strong date. Top half is weak. There are also several interesting die breaks of this date and mintmark. One starts at Miss Liberty's feet and runs all the way to the rim. Some of the die breaks give you the false illusion of the overdate, such as 1918, 1918, 1918, or over some other part of date. This date is more readily available than some of the better known keys and semi-key dates, such as 1923-S, 1921, 1919-D, 1919-S, and 1927-S, but not with Full Heads.

One of the worst for any eagle's breast feathers of all of the Standing Liberty Quarters. They come with little detail or none at all. Also, Miss Liberty's gown is weak in her thigh area, which explains, in part, the weakness on the eagle's breast on the reverse. Frequently comes "dirty" looking, also as though it had dirt in the dies-thus some are very porous. Miss Liberty's thigh to her waist is frequently softly struck, or even incused, and may have a nice Full Head on this date and mint mark. Strangely enough, when this happens (when the coin is uncirculated), it is usually toned a reddish or even coppery tone. Comes dish struck, or deeply struck with a wire rim, but still weak in the torso. Many available in M.S. 65 grade, but weak.

On the obverse, Miss Liberty's knee and right thigh are also very weakly struck, as well as the rivets on the shield; especially the last four on the left side. Needless to say, most have flat heads. Full Heads should command 5 to 10 times present Guidebook prices.

GRADING:

OBVERSE

Since all of the above has been said concerning the date and the mintmarks, some relaxing of normal grading standards should prevail in most grades. Keep this in mind for top circulated grades: Rivets missing from shield. Weak mid-section on Miss Liberty.

REVERSE

Weakly struck. Almost no breast feathers is the order of the day on this one, even on the Uncirculated pieces. Examine this one carefully.

* * *

AVAILABILITY OF FULL HEADS:

		MS65	MS66	MS67
FULL HEADS:	PCGS	23	6	0
	NGC	8	2	0
NON-FULL HEADS:				
	PCGS	32	7	0
	NGC	16	7	2

I certainly have seen a host of 1918-D's in Full Head holders (from both major services) that would not part this man from his money! Mostly MS64 FH and MS65 FH. The scenario is usually the same: lacks a bit in the temple area, or just barely makes the minimum FH description as outlined elsewhere in the book.

There are some monster Sharp Full Heads (or Ultimate Full Heads) in this date and mintmark that should command much more money than the "standard" Full Heads. I certainly hope this comment does not confuse - it's intended to help clear up the FH dilemma. I hope the grading services will add Sharp Full Head (SFH) and Ultimate Full Head (UFH) to the description on the holder. It would help with a more accurate description, as the PL and DMPL designations on Morgan Dollars. The S.L.Q.C.S. club approached me and asked if I would be on a panel that would address the possibility of calling Full Heads on quarters: "A,B,C,D,E,F Heads". I thought that breakdown was too confusing but still feel that SFH for sharp and UFH for ultimate would help. Naturally, these designations would command a much higher premium that the regular Full Heads at time of sale.

#C-5115. Very interesting die breaks. In the past, this was considered to be a variety of the 1918/7-S. But obviously is <u>not</u> an overdate.

#C-5116. This piece was purchased very early in my collecting life and this too was thought to be the 1918/7-D and is indeed the closest to the overdate of a 1918-D I have ever seen. But it is not an overdate.

1918-S

Mintage: 11,072,000

Price Rank—9
Quantity Rank—30

G	VG	F	VF	XF	AU	BU	GEM
10%	15%	15%	20%	15%	15%	5%	5%

3% STRUCK WITH FULL HEADS

Probably less than three percent of these were struck with real Full Heads. Yet there are many 1918-S's in higher grades (VF to AU). The reason being, the "S" mint has always been the magic mintmark; the scarce one; the one to keep. Most collectors kept the "S" mints out, when found in circulation. Full Heads of this date are VERY, VERY scarce.

With so many flat heads of this date and especially with the mintage as high as it is, the dies were used well beyond their normal life expectancy. At this particular time, the American public was clamoring for more minor coins, since things were booming and the need was great. All minting facilities were running at full capacity. This year was the largest amount of "S" mint quarters produced at the San Francisco mint. This, of course, explains why there were so many flat heads.

In grading the 1918-S, due consideration must be given, as Full Heads are worth many times the current Coin Dealers Newsletter pricing guide, or the Redbook prices, which most people use as a guideline. A trait of the 1918-S in CH.BU, GEM or original, is that they always look "dirty" That is some dirt or darkness in the devices. This date does come with Full Head and all ten toes.

The coin pictured above is almost in a class by itself. THE finest I have ever seen. "Head and shoulders" above any I have seen in 35 years in collecting Standing Liberty Quarters. The photo does not do justice to the coin.

A variety of die breaks exist of the 1918-S. Have examined many that come close at first-but only a die break in the date. Some die breaks run vertical and horizontal. The closest is a die break very slightly to the right of the "8" giving the appearance of an overdate.

GRADING:

OBVERSE

Frequently weak and easy to buy AU's as Uncirculated. DON'T!! Light wear is not to be confused with weak strikes. Weak strikes have NO skid lines (many lines going in several directions). Most rivets on shield are missing. Weak chain mail. Most have only 50-60% head.

REVERSE

Weak, at best. Missing feathers, especially on left wing on most pieces.

* * *

AVAILABILITY OF FULL HEADS:

		MS65	MS66	MS67
FULL HEADS:	PCGS	10	0	0
	NGC	5	0	1
NON-FULL HEADS:				
	PCGS	24	10	0
	NGC	27	7	1

Sharp Full Heads on pieces from both services have been handled and placed by our offices. Light to medium golden, and most looked as though they were struck from the same die. The one MS67 FH graded by N.G.C. was sold in 1992 in a Superior Auction sale, but was a buy-back. (Maybe too close to P.C.G.S. "territory"?) Still, in all, it was a beautiful coin. The non-Full Head MS67 piece is so immaculate, but not quite a Full Head. It is light golden and rose, and bagmark free and living in Florida.

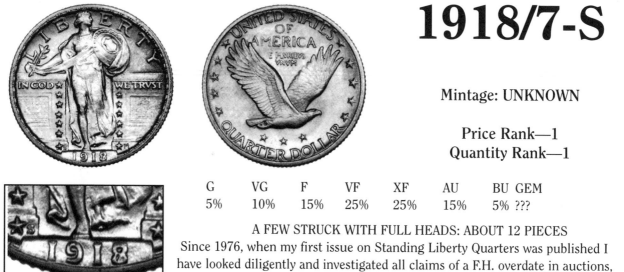

1918/7-S

Mintage: UNKNOWN

Price Rank—1
Quantity Rank—1

G	VG	F	VF	XF	AU	BU GEM
5%	10%	15%	25%	25%	15%	5% ???

A FEW STRUCK WITH FULL HEADS: ABOUT 12 PIECES

Since 1976, when my first issue on Standing Liberty Quarters was published I have looked diligently and investigated all claims of a F.H. overdate in auctions, sales catalogues, and private sales all to no avail.

The coin pictured surfaced in Corpus Christi, Texas and is the finest I have ever seen of a Full Head specimen and an M.S. 65/65.

This overdate was caused by the recutting of a 1917 die. This recutting was practiced by all mints in the late 1880's to 1890's; especially the silver dollars, such as the 1879 over 80, 1880-O over S,1900-O over CC, Etc. This list is almost endless.

When a die was left over from previous years, rather than throw it away, it was reworked with the next year's date. Not a dual hubbing, as this would result in doubled obverse or reverse, or both. Another modification that was practiced liberally during the Turban Half series (1808-1836) was modifying the dies from years past to be used for the striking of a later year. This practice was supposed to have been abandoned around the turn of the century, but once in a while it is still practiced (such as 1954-D/S Jefferson Nickel); which usually results in a very low mintage and as usual, there are a few that are reworked. The life of a normal die is only a few thousand (estimated from 3,000 to 15,000) and the life expectancy from a reworked die is considerably less, because the date breaks away. This is still practiced today. I have personally talked to retiring Andrea Zungalow of the U.S. Mint, and she confirms this.

The first appearance of the overdate at public auction was the Barney Bluestone sale on December 4, 1937, as Lot #741. It sold for the unheard of figure of $26.25. The coin was brilliant uncirculated. It was thought at the time to be unique, but not so!

Though the 1918/7-S first appeared in the Standard Catalog in 1942, it was discovered many years before (1937) and the variety was not discovered until many years after its mintage.

The 1918/7-S overdate was caused by die alterations and as with all overdates, they are very weakly struck on the breast, thigh, shield, and head.

It is rumored that there is the possibility of a 1918/7-P and also D, by at least one Mid-west dealer. But to date, nothing has come to the front concerning their existence and we can only say there possibly exist overdates of Denver and Philadelphia in 1918 also.

There are several ways to tell the genuine from the counterfeit of this date and mintmark.

#1 The most common counterfeits are castings. In this case, look for little piles of metal in the fields that would usually be flat. Similar to grains of sand under magnification.

#2 Genuine pieces have the "E" clash from reverse at right knee of Miss Liberty.

#3 Your author likes the broken die or eagle's wing clash, running through the "T" of "Trust" on the obverse.

#4 There are also many die polish marks on the reverse around "AME" of "America" and in the field behind the eagle's right wing (as you face coin) on genuine pieces.

#5 Also on the 1918/7-S, one of the classic die varieties for substantiation is: A broken die beginning at the rim at about two o'clock (or at the "T" of "Liberty." It runs down through the rim on the obverse, through the first crossbar of the T in "Liberty," connecting the first crossbar to the upright of the "T" and stopping at the bottom of the "T." This is easily discernible with a 10X magnifier. This is not true of all 1918/7-S's, but just another interesting point on many genuine pieces.

#6 The step under Miss Liberty's left foot is missing and usually her toes also.

Although some do not consider the overdate a part of the set, your author considers that any date struck by the mint, overdate or not, is needed to complete the set. Since this was done at the mint and was not an error. It was planned.

While we are on the subject, all of the overdates with a full head that I have examined have a broken die resulting in a raised line on Miss Liberty's throat. It runs from the middle of her left breast to the bottom of her ear lobe. This is true of all the overdates I have examined in full head, and I have examined all but one piece to date.

GRADING:

OBVERSE

All were struck with working dies, so virtually none exist in M.S. 65/65 Full Head. Just a little wear, and most would call this a VF or XF, when in reality it is an AU. Characteristically weak in the knee, head, shield. Rarely any lines in shield, vertical or horizontal. Several rivets missing.

REVERSE

Rarely does the eagle come with any breast feathers. Usually, the eagle's right wing will be bare and/or flat.

*Author's note: I examined a 1918/17-S at the Long Beach show in June 1986 that was a casting. Had all the attributes and characteristics of the real thing, but POROUS SURFACES. Even the numbers of the date were rounded. Coin was only VF or so. Had all clashes to verify-but NO GOOD.

*   *   *

AVAILABILITY OF FULL HEADS:

		MS63	MS64	MS65	MS66	MS67
FULL HEADS:	PCGS	1	1	0	0	0
	NGC	1	1	0	0	0
NON-FULL HEADS:						
	PCGS	7	14	1	2	0
	NGC	2	11	1	0	0

Without any debate, the 1918/7-S Standing Liberty Quarter is the very rarest full head in the entire series. None in MS65, MS66, or MS67 FH. Head and shoulders rarer than any other date, including the 1927-S. I have submitted and had encapsulated, purchased and sold all of the full heads, with the exception of the P.C.G.S. MS60 FH piece. That piece was offered for sale to me in Overland, Kansas at the Central States Numismatic Society convention in 1990. I did not agree with the mint state designation assigned to the coin, as it looked as though it had been lost in a gravel parking lot and "banged-up" plenty! That is why I did not purchase the piece.

The ultimate full head for an overdate has to be the N.G.C. MS64 FH piece. It has the sharpest full head I have seen on an overdate. Coin is light golden and mostly satiny; well-matched obverse and reverse. It has the characteristic die break down Miss Liberty's throat (raised line), but an outstanding full head! A great strike overall. The coin is in strong hands in Florida.

The piece in the 1990 Boys Town Sale by Superior - MS66, P.C.G.S. encapsulated, Lot #3727 was very flashy, but with no semblance of a head. The N.G.C. MS63 FH has the characteristic die break down the throat from Miss Liberty's chin to the top of her gown (on all of the pieces I have placed), and this piece lives out West.

The P.C.G.S./N.G.C. MS64 FH is ONE coin. The collector who has this piece still has the P.C.G.S. insert, as it is currently in the N.G.C. holder. It, too, has the die break (with a slightly raised line) at the throat and the P.C.G.S. AU 58 FH has this same characteristic as well. I know of only one other piece that is not encapsulated, and that piece would probably grade an AU 55-58. In 1980, I also purchased a raw full head overdate at the A.N.A. Apostrophe Sale, in the Stack's section. I shipped it to a customer in New York and it was lost by the U.S. Post Office, along with six other goodies - one of the goodies was a 1919-D with a sharp full head. These pieces were all raw and this occurred before the grading services opened their doors.

1919

Mintage: 11,324,000

Price Rank—29
Quantity Rank—33

G	VG	F	VF	XF	AU	BU	GEM
5%	10%	10%	10%	10%	15%	20%	20%

25% STRUCK WITH FULL HEADS

The 1919 is a date you may call "common" in uncirculated condition; if you can call any date of Standing Liberty Quarters "common", especially before 1925. It has a high mintage and is one of the most available with a Full Head in the teens. It is also the second piece for which your author paid a premium for a Full Head. ($12.50: the flat heads were selling for $10.00).

With the exception of the first digit, this date is usually stronger struck than other dates.

It is in print by another author as a scarce coin-but, NOT SO. Having followed and collected Standing Liberty Quarters for some thirty-five years, your author parallels the coin with the 1930 for Full Heads, though the 1930 is a bit more common than the 1919. They are closely related in availability of Full Heads and probably 20% were originally struck with Full Heads.

Authors Note: In 1985,1 examined many of this date and mintmark that were castings. The high mintage may be the reason no one would suspect. Not all were uncirculated. Many were as low as VF or XF. As with most castings-it had a granular surface and with a 10 power or greater magnifying glass was discernable to the trained eye.

Lots of Full Heads; but do not make the mistake of comparing it with the 1919-D or S. UNFAIR!! About 3,000 miles apart geographically speaking. Also in strike.

GRADING:

OBVERSE

A very strong strike. Should grade top of scale for pre-'25 Standing Liberty Quarters. Also most common pre-'25 for Full Heads except the 1917 type 1. Full Heads come as low as XF.

REVERSE

Most always strong and many feathers on eagle's wing and breast. Usually, pin feathers on outer parts of wings as well.

* * *

AVAILABILITY OF FULL HEADS:

		MS65	MS66	MS67	MS68
FULL HEADS:	PCGS	46	20	4	1
	NGC	24	24	3	0
NON-FULL HEADS:					
	PCGS	67	51	3	0
	NGC	63	22	4	0

With over 11,000,000 pieces struck, this is not an overly exciting date and mintmark. There are many real "screamers," both Sharp Full Head and Ultimate Full Head in both services. The piece that sold in the 1990 Father Flanagan's Boys Home Sale by Superior Galleries was incredibly white and a Sharp, Full Head. The MS67 FH pieces that I have placed over the years meet all of the Full Head criteria and are sharp, too.

The Ultimate Full Head and the most outstanding piece of the series is the MS68 FH: a 1919 PCGS. The coin is blast white and virtually perfect in every respect! The description in Superior's January, 1994 catalog of the Rothenberger sale reads: "Wow! Wait until you see this coin; it is absolutely, utterly, gorgeous. So flashy is it, and so fresh, that we would not be surprised to hear specialists say after the sale that it is the finest Standing Liberty Quarter of them all. (Indeed, there are only 4 Mint State 68s FH in the entire roster of 38 dates and mints.) Do not miss the chance of examining it beforehand. If you fail to, you will have the rest of time to regret your inaction."

There is a 1924 MS68 PCGS, but it is not a FH. So, at this time there are 4 pieces in MS68 FH (Knoxville pieces are three of this number) and the lone 1919: 68 FH at PCGS.

1919-D

Mintage: 1,944,000

Price Rank—8
Quantity Rank—14

G	VG	F	VF	XF	AU	BU	GEM
8%	10%	20%	20%	15%	15%	7%	5%

1% STRUCK WITH FULL HEADS

This date is one of the most underrated dates and mintmarks in the whole series in M.S. 65/67, Full Head. Its true rarity is more than the 1916. Many collectors kept the "S" mint as they were produced, but not so with the "D" mint. Collecting by year and mintmark did not become really popular until Wayet Raymond began putting out the "Blue Savers Board" in the middle thirties. This was a cardboard, wall-hung board into which the coins were pressed, though some collectors put the completed collection into a frame with glass.

The date is characteristically weak and Miss Liberty's head is most always flat. The rivets on the shield on the left side are usually obscured or obliterated completely. Like its sister (1918-D) coin there are many interesting die breaks on the obverse around the date. Perhaps during the war years, the silver was not properly alloyed or the dies were hurried out for lack of time.

There are many that have an incused area on the shield or upper half of the date. This was done at the mint. The area is well rounded and shiny, but not furrowed, as would be the case if it was not a mint problem. Most likely the mint employee installing the die "bumped" the finished die on the alignment pins or a slightly, rounded object, thus making a dent in the new die. The lines in the shield (vertical and horizontal) are usually sharp and complete when this happens. Especially around the "bumped" area.

GRADING:

OBVERSE
Usually much weaker strike than 1919-S. Chain mail, shield and torso. The tendency is to downgrade this coin. Usually the 3rd and 4th rivets are missing from the shield also.

REVERSE
Much weaker here, too. Especially on the eagle's breast feathers.

* * *

AVAILABILITY OF FULL HEADS:

		MS65	MS66	MS67
FULL HEADS:	PCGS	3	4	0
	NGC	1	1	0
NON-FULL HEADS:				
	PCGS	26	20	0
	NGC	14	6	0

    1919-D is one of the major keys of the series, and high-end Full Head pieces are very rare. N.G.C. has only slabbed 1 piece in MS65 FH and one piece in MS66 FH. Until the 1/2 roll surfaced in California a few years ago, they had only slabbed 2 pieces of MS65 FH and 1 piece of MS66 FH. No MS67 FH or non-full head in either service. WOW! How rare!! It has long been common knowledge that there are fewer 1919-D FH pieces than 1919-S MS65-up FH's. I have found homes for both the MS65 FH and MS66 FH pieces from NGC and have placed several of the PCGS MS65 FH and MS66 FH's. It seems that when a true MS FH 1919-D surfaces, it is in the category of Sharp Full Head or Ultimate Full Head.

    I shipped a super piece to New York in 1980, that was lost by the good old U.S. Mail (yes, it was registered, but still was lost). I had to bring suit against the Post Office. I had registered the package for $150,000 and paid the fee to obtain insurance for that amount from the Post Office, but they claimed they were only liable for $25,000. After 2 years of litigation, I had to write off the $125,000 on my taxes. It hurt, but was not disastrous. Now, the U.S. Post Office states on their page of Registry Fees: "Fees for articles valued over $25,000 are for handling only. $25,000 is the maximum amount of insurance coverage available". They then list values of $25,000-15,000,000 and make unit charges for each $1,000 increment of value. The quoted statement regarding $25,000 limit did not appear in the publications/manuals in 1980 when the loss occurred. The only good that came of the litigation and expense on my part was that the Post Office now has it in print that they will not pay over $25,000 per loss.

1919-S

Mintage: 1,836,000

Price Rank—5
Quantity Rank—12

G	VG	F	VF	XF	AU	BU	GEM
5%	10%	20%	20%	25%	10%	5%	5%

2% STRUCK WITH FULL HEADS

The 1919-S has long been considered one of the key coins of the series among most collectors and dealers. The 1919-D and 1919-S are usually paralleled in price and rarity.

Full Heads of this date are very rare and would be closely paralleled with the value of the 1916 and very difficult to locate.

This is one of those dates on which your author questions the mintage figures. In this particular date and mintmark, I would guess the mintage figures are somewhat over the amount actually produced, or an exceptional amount of these got the dates worn off before collectors were aware of their scarcity. This statement is made after more than 40 years of researching and collecting.

If you think some Standing Liberty Quarters are not a good investment, compare my first book (Page 133) or the Coin Dealer Newsletter 6/11/76 to the current information. This coin was valued at $750.00 M.S. 65, Full Head in 1976. WOW!!! Current Greysheet: $10,000/11,000 but Trends at $30,000!

*Author's Note: A word of caution on this date and mintmark. I examined a casting of the 1919-S at the Illinois State show in 1984. As is the rule of all castings, look for granular surfaces. Also the outer rim was doubled. Coin had the appearance of a circulated coin, but the date was that of an uncirculated coin. CANNOT BE!! Date is the highest part of coin.

GRADING:

OBVERSE

Normally the "S" mint in a given year is weak when compared to the "D". However, this is not the case in 1919. Normal weakness persists, both obverse and reverse. Again, rivets are missing from shield. Lines in shield are shallow. Gown lacks sharp details.

REVERSE

Normal weakness in eagle's breast feathers and eagle's right wing.

* * *

AVAILABILITY OF FULL HEADS:

		MS65	MS66	MS67
FULL HEADS:	PCGS	7	1	1
	NGC	6	0	1
NON-FULL HEADS:				
	PCGS	15	4	0
	NGC	14	4	0

The MS66 FH was an upgrade from an MS65 FH, and I agree that it should have graded MS66 FH the first time. It lives out West, and the other thirteen pieces in MS65 FH (total of both services) are scattered throughout this beautiful country. I have placed quite a few of them in their present homes, with both collectors and speculators. At this writing, only one piece is on the market in a P.C.G.S. holder and one piece is on the market in an N.G.C. holder.

The Boys Town Sale MS67 FH was a super piece from the word "go"! An ultimate full head, bright white and one of the most gorgeous pieces I have ever seen in this series. The hammer came down at $42,000.00 plus the 10% buyer's premium.

1919-S is a long time key in the series, as well as the magic mintmark with only three pieces in MS66 FH and MS67 FH total at both grading services. NO full heads in MS68 at either P.C.G.S. or N.G.C.

1920

Mintage: 27,860,000

Price Rank—23
Quantity Rank—38

G	VG	F	VF	XF	AU	BU	GEM
10%	10%	10%	15%	15%	10%	20%	10%

10% STRUCK WITH FULL HEADS

This date has many die breaks, though the date is usually strong. Most die breaks are on the obverse and mostly around the date, but the digit "1" in the date is usually strong. There are some exceptions to this. The "1" of the date does occasionally come very weak (a faint outline only). The one pictured here is the exception. It almost looks like a Type III (1926 and later) when the date was recessed.

This date more than doubles the next highest mintage. With a high mintage, more new dies are used, and with each new die, several Full Head pieces should follow. Strangely, there seem to be LESS Full Heads of this date than there are of the 1919, with a little over 11,000,000 minted (not even half the mintage of this piece). This further proves a former conclusion that the new dies did not receive proper hardening attention, or tempering, so they did not last as they should, especially in the head area where most stress occurs.

GRADING:

OBVERSE

Some real "mind blowers" exist of this date and mintmark. Many nice, sharp Full Heads (sharp separation from hairline and face). Second only to the 1919 in availability of Full Heads. Many are frosty.

REVERSE

Most always strong including the edge of the eagle's right wing.

*Author's Note: Same as the 1919-P. I have seen many castings in the past year of this date and mintmark. Have found several in lower grades (VF-XF) as well. Again, look for granular surfaces using a 10x or greater glass.

* * *

AVAILABILITY OF FULL HEADS:

		MS65	MS66	MS67
FULL HEADS:	PCGS	46	4	0
	NGC	19	3	0
NON-FULL HEADS:				
	PCGS	107	7	0
	NGC	66	27	4

With a mintage nearly double that of the next highest mintage (the 1918), you would think the Full Head numbers would be very different. However, there are NO MS67 FH pieces and only four MS67 non-full head pieces! One of the "nons" lives in Florida and is nearly a full head, but no cigar. I have handled several of the MS66 FH's; a couple of which barely make the FH grade with minimum detail requirements. The ones remaining are nice, sharp full heads.

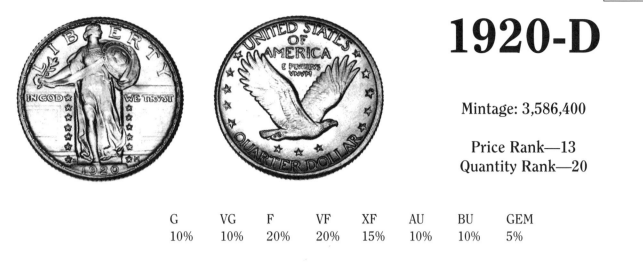

1920-D

Mintage: 3,586,400

Price Rank—13
Quantity Rank—20

G	VG	F	VF	XF	AU	BU	GEM
10%	10%	20%	20%	15%	10%	10%	5%

5% STRUCK WITH FULL HEADS

The 1920-D is one of those dates that sneaks up on you. The mintage would indicate a very common date, but not so. Very underrated on today's market. It ranks 20th in mintage; and true Full Heads are not plentiful by any stretch of the imagination. Like so many of the Standing Liberty Quarters, this date is also usually weakly struck. Your author rates this coin closely parallel to the 1921, 1919-D, and 1919-S in uncirculated condition. Again, if mintage figures were to be challenged, this date would be one to be challenged. This coin, in Full Head, M.S. 65/67, would be worth at least five times or more present Guidebook prices.

Many of the 1920's have the upper half of the date very weakly struck as though the die was clogged or broken out, or struck through cloth or paper or some other foreign material in the die.

Numerous die breaks exist of this date-especially from East to West and through much of the top of the date, and down halfway into the date. Never in the lower half of the date.

GRADING:

OBVERSE

This date and mintmark was struck very weakly, especially in the leg, thigh, and lower torso. Upper half of the date was weak from the beginning. Frequently 3rd and 4th rivets are missing from shield. Last star is weak, also. VF, XF, and AU- relax on grading. Do not use the full date on this one to call it a VF or better.

REVERSE

A little better strike than the obverse, though frequently not all feathers show on the eagle's breast and wings-especially the ones on the front edge of his wings (usually missing). Consider the whole coin when grading all circulated coins of this date and mintmark.

* * *

AVAILABILITY OF FULL HEADS:

		MS65	MS66	MS67
FULL HEADS:	PCGS	19	3	3
	NGC	4	0	2
NON-FULL HEADS:				
	PCGS	22	11	0
	NGC	9	5	0

I have placed all three of the P.C.G.S MS67 FH's, and would have to rate the piece that resides in Virginia as the finest head; not only of the 1920-D's, but of any Standing Liberty Quarter. The tuft of hair (ear lobe area) below the full head is sharp and rounded. It is a bright coin with only a touch of light golden toning and is outstanding in every respect, with no distracting bagmarks. * The N.G.C. piece I placed has no bagmarks either and is overall exceptional in every respect - even seems a bit underrated to me. Some like blast white and some like toning, and that is the only difference between these two pieces.

With only eight pieces in MS66 FH and MS67 FH, there can only be eight outstanding sets in the world at this point in time.

* While writing this revision, N.G.C. encapsulated the second piece in MS67 FH. Lovely toning, but not as nice as the first piece mentioned above. The second piece has a few faint bagmarks on Miss Liberty's right leg, and resides in the far west.

1920-S

Mintage: 6,380,000

Price Rank—3
Quantity Rank—25

G	VG	F	VF	XF	AU	BU	GEM
10%	15%	15%	20%	15%	10%	10%	5%

2% OR LESS STRUCK WITH FULL HEADS

Pictured above is the finest known of this date and mintmark. l have eagerly sought this coin in CH.BU, M.S. 65/67, Full Head, and since the writing of the original book (1976) none have come close. l have been offered many times Greysheet bid for this coin. This date and mintmark is the classic underrated coin in the whole series, especially M.S. 63 and up, and Full Head.

The 1920-S is a very rare item in true Full Head. It should be valued many times over Redbook price. Your author gives a rate of 2nd or 3rd in value of the entire series. It is always a weak strike in both obverse and reverse. Very much underrated. The same is true of this "S" mint as is with most other "S" mints-weak dies; soft strikes. This is a trait that carries over into the half, dime and nickel in the same year. It seems as though this is the advent of the weak strike "S" mints that carried throughout most of the 1920's.

GRADING:

OBVERSE

Much, much weaker than you would expect. Weak in rivets on shield, head, toes, vertical and horizontal lines in shield. Gown lines and chain mail are weak on most. All in all, quite miserably struck. Look at entire coin when grading, and "if in doubt, don't".

REVERSE

Same rule applies as obverse. Weak. All feathers on eagle's breast may be there, but soft or "mushy". Center breast may have no feathers.

* * *

AVAILABILITY OF FULL HEADS:

		MS64	MS65	MS66	MS67
FULL HEADS:	PCGS	3	3	3	0
	NGC	4	3	0	0
NON-FULL HEADS:					
	PCGS	48	21	6	0
	NGC	31	18	1	1

If you include the MS64 FH pieces from both services (and we have) you still only have seven pieces at N.G.C. and nine at P.C.G.S. These pieces command about one-half the price of an MS65 FH. In the top grades of MS65 FH, MS66 FH, you will have a total of only nine pieces. I further suspect that a tab or two have not been returned to the grading service to correct this number.

I placed the finest of the MS66 FH's and have seen the other two P.C.G.S. pieces. The first was light golden and the second did not even come close to the other pieces in my opinion. Of the MS65 FH pieces, I have found homes for two of the six pieces and they do have sharp full heads.

There is one obverse die for this date and mintmark that is strong, and it seems that all of the full head 1920-S's were probably struck from the same die.

#C-5195

1920-S Teardrop

In late 1994 I found a new variety - that is a 1920-S tear-drop. Unfortunately, the coin was in a lower grade, VG/F. Unlike the 1926-S tear-drop which is located closer to the side than to Miss Liberty's left leg, this 1920-S tear-drop is a bit smaller and very close to her left leg. The shape is that of a tear that has run just a bit - very much like the 1926-S. (A side note for those who might not know just how a tear-drop occurs in our modern minting facilities: The working die either breaks away or a fragment of metal from a foreign source gets into the collar or on the blank planchet. When the die strikes the coin, that foreign material causes the die to chip or break, thus leaving a chipped out depression in the die. Then on subsequent strikes of that die, the metal raises up into that die depression causing, in this case, the tear-drop of metal appearing along the side of Miss Liberty's leg.)

I did see one other 1920-S tear-drop MANY years ago and I thought an article would appear in Coin World and/or MacNeil's Notes. But... there are only so many hours in a day for each of us. 24 hours is enough some days - but on others, I could use 36 or so!

So, look carefully at your 1920-S's (as well as your 1926-S's) for the "famed" tear-drop. There does seem to be a strong demand for these interesting pieces!

* * *

AVAILABILITY OF FULL HEADS:

FULL HEADS:		MS65	MS66	MS67
	PCGS	?	?	?
	NGC	?	?	?
NON-FULL HEADS:				
	PCGS	?	?	?
	NGC	?	?	?

#C-5195.
Close-up of teardrop.

This one of the very obvious teardrops of the series. The 1926-S was the first one discovered and remains the classic. The 1920-S is one of the more recent discoveries. A piece of the die broke away at Miss Liberty's left leg about half way down. The coins struck after that break look like a teardrop beside Miss Liberty's leg. Some call it a cud.

This is a much sought after piece by most collectors who have a complete set.

1921

Mintage: 1,916,000

Price Rank—16
Quantity Rank—13

G	VG	F	VF	XF	AU	BU	GEM
5%	5%	30%	20%	10%	10%	10%	10%

5% STRUCK WITH FULL HEADS

The 1921 is a low mintage and long considered a key coin of the series. Consequently, it has been a popular coin through out the years. Nice, uncirculated specimens are not easy to come by-but much easier than the 1920-S.

There are some incredible strikes of this date. Wire rim; full, rounded sharp head with the three olive leaves on Miss Liberty's head complete from top to bottom. Deeply struck into planchet-perhaps one of the dies was cut smaller by just a few thousandths of a inch and made the planchet appear oversized; thus a much stronger than normal strike.

The 1921 has a tendency to be somewhat better struck than other years before and after 1921.

It seems that when the Walking Liberty Half was modified in 1921, the quarter was also modified to some extent. When compared to other dates of the Standing Liberty Quarters, the detail of the 1921 is very sharp and many outstanding pieces of this date do exist. Unlike the earlier Standing Liberty Quarters, the 1921 was often struck weak at the lower half of the date, further proving that the dies were modified. The 1920-P is exactly reversed from this. On many of these Type I's, the reed and bead from about 3 o'clock to 8 o'clock is frequently flatly struck.

Having been struck in the "roaring '20's", many coins were saved and found their way into circulation during the "Great Depression"; but only circulated for a short time. This accounts in part, at least, for these numerous high grades in this year.

Incredible strikes command a much stronger price than "bid" or "ask". When I say this, I mean 1 1/2 to 2 times "bid", depending on how badly you want the coin.

GRADING:

OBVERSE

Seem to be two types of this date and mintmark. Type I: struck before die modification. Most of these are weak, overall. Type II: Outstanding. Full, sharp head, sharp full lines in shield. Deeply struck or "dish effect". Nearly always sharp gown lines, olive branch leaves, and berries. Even clapboards are sharp.

REVERSE

Same criteria as obverse.

*Author's Note: Strange phenomenon about the AU's of this date. True AU's are few and far between and MOST have been cleaned. WHY???

* * *

AVAILABILITY OF FULL HEADS:

		MS65	MS66	MS67
FULL HEADS:	PCGS	26	3	0
	NGC	13	1	0
NON-FULL HEADS:				
	PCGS	44	10	0
	NGC	25	2	0

The Full Head 1921's are usually "there" and sharp, but some of the early grading was a bit optimistic on the Full Head description. I have seen approximately 6 pieces that I would not call Full Heads using today's criteria - this from both service. There are two types of 1921's in my opinion. When the modification was done of the Walking Liberty Halves and Mercury Dimes, I believe some modification was also made to the dies of the Standing Liberty Quarters. Consequently, the "type 2" 1921 can come with a screamer head (Ultimate Full Head) and most pieces I have seen in Full Head holders are the Type 2. I disagree with the grading of 2 of the MS66 FH's; they are nice MS65 FH's in my eyes. We tried to get one crossed over into an NGC holder, and obviously they agreed with me, as it did not cross.

The 1921 and 1923-S have long run a race as to which is the rarer piece. It now appears that the 1921 is a good bit more scarce, particularly in MS65 FH and MS66 FH. PCGS has slabbed 26 pcs. in MS65 FH; NGC has slabbed 13. PCGS has slabbed 3 pcs. in MS66 FH; NGC has done 1. On the 1923-S: PCGS - 25 MS65 FH's. NGC - 14 MS65 FH's. PCGS - 9 MS66 FH's, NGC - 6 MS FH's.

There are only 4 MS66 FH 1921's, compared to 15 MS66 FH 1923-S's! Also, it is very possible that this is one of the dates where not all of the broken-out inserts were returned.

1923

Mintage: 9,716,000

Price Rank—19
Quantity Rank—29

G	VG	F	VF	XF	AU	BU	GEM
20%	10%	10%	20%	10%	10%	10%	10%

10% STRUCK WITH FULL HEADS

This date seems to be struck very broad. That is, the figures that make up the date appear as though they were flattened after the die was made-or polished down to some extent. Perhaps this was done in an effort to get dates to wear better and also to take away some of the stress in hopes that they would not break out as they had so often in the teens. This has already been discussed in other parts of this book; i.e. 1918-D.

When compared to the 1923-S the date is needle sharp in the "9" and the bottom part of the "3". (See explanation on 1923-S). Frequently comes with a "dirty face". The entire obverse of the coin sometimes appears as though there were some dust or dirt particles in the die that were impressed into the coin surfaces when the coin was struck.

Frequently the temple area is weak or non existing on some that are slabbed Full Head. Look this point over very carefully in this area. Much scarcer than previously thought in Full Head.

GRADING:

This date and mintmark can be had in what is called a "screamer" or a "monster" coin. In other words, an outstanding strike, both in head, shield, and toes. Many have a satiny finish and a strong Full Head. Generally, this coin should meet normal grading standards.

OBVERSE
Usually well struck, but 50% or better are weak around the date.

REVERSE
Usually as strong or stronger than most "P" mints, pre-1925. Nice breast feathers.

* * *

J.H. Cline   93

AVAILABILITY OF FULL HEADS:

		MS65	MS66	MS67
FULL HEADS:	PCGS	15	7	0
	NGC	15	4	0
NON-FULL HEADS:				
	PCGS	216	111	5
	NGC	187	67	7

When the grading services began, they used the description that read..... "including the 3 olive leaves in Miss Liberty's Hair" for the full head designation. That probably should be a bit relaxed on the 1923, since the line separating Miss Liberty's cheek, jawbone and ear hole is all there but the horizontal leaf above that line is frequently flat. I disagree with possibly as many as one half of the pieces that are in MS65 FH and MS66 FH holders and feel that they should not be FH. There are also MANY in non-full head holders that should be encapsulated "FH". The normal scenario is for the line separating Miss Liberty's cheek, forehead and jaw to be a bit lacking in the temple area.

1923-S

Mintage: 1,360,000

Price Rank—18
Quantity Rank—6

G	VG	F	VF	XF	AU	BU	GEM
10%	15%	10%	25%	15%	15%	5%	5%

5% STRUCK WITH FULL HEADS

The 1923-S for a long time has been one of the key coins of the series, being sixth in quantity and eighteenth in pricing. It proves most collectors and dealers are aware of this key date.

Many Full Heads M.S. 60/60 and M.S. 63/63's of this date and mintmark exist. Full M.S. 65/65's with Full Head are scarce, but they are out there. Takes a lot of perseverance. When a 1923-S with M.S. 65/65 Full Head comes up in an auction it usually sets new records with the price realized.Some have the Ultimate Full Head, but are usually slabbed in MS66FH.

Some attempts have been made at altering the 1928-S but, of course, the 1928-S is recessed under the top step and very easily detectable-even by most beginners.

In the last few years, I have seen this coin with an added mintmark more than all other dates combined. In comparing this mintmark with the 1923-P: the "2" of the date is fat at the base and half way down the curve of the "2". The 1923-P "2" is needle sharp and very thin. I looked at an added mintmark at a Florida dealer's table at a coin convention and convinced him it was NO GOOD. Just as I walked away, he said "I am still going to sell it and get my money back out of it. Let the man who buys it decide for himself." So, DO BE INFORMED. The 1923 date is thin. The genuine 1923-S date is fat.

Frequently harder to locate than the 1916, particularly in VF through AU.

GRADING:

OBVERSE

Above the average for "S" mints. Lots of AU pieces on the market are being bought and sold as BU. Flattened chain mail is a dead give-away for any wear. Also any flattening on knee and inner shield. Again-look for a brown cast and "if in doubt- don't". Get a second opinion.

REVERSE

Medium to well struck. Should meet normal grading criteria from most Standing Liberty Quarters (not 1917-P Ty. I)

* * *

AVAILABILITY OF FULL HEADS:

		MS65	MS66	MS67
FULL HEADS:	PCGS	26	8	0
	NGC	16	8	0
NON-FULL HEADS:				
	PCGS	61	12	1
	NGC	25	11	1

Most , if not all, of the MS66 FH's have been seen by yours truly and I have placed many of them. I can remember three pieces in P.C.G.S. holders and two in N.G.C. holders with which I did not agree on the full head designation. In each instance, I felt they were MS65 non-full head. Perhaps the early grading?

I sent in a Standing Liberty quarter to one of the grading services when they were removing toning in special cases. They returned it to me with a note stating that the toning was a part of the coin's grade. I guess they know something I don't know. I have seen at least ten other pieces in MS65 FH with which I don't agree - neither the MS nor the FH. When I do not agree with the grade assigned by the service, I do not handle the coin.

Since the inception of the major grading services in 1986, they have proven that the 1921 is a bit more scarce than the 1923-S; particularly in MS65 FH and MS66 FH.

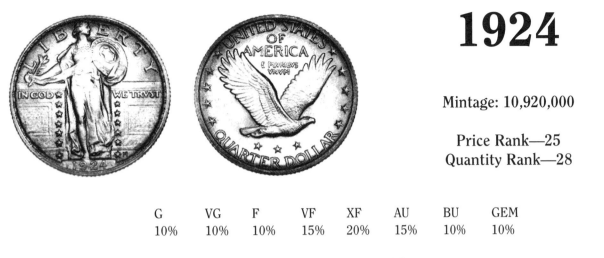

1924

Mintage: 10,920,000

Price Rank—25
Quantity Rank—28

G	VG	F	VF	XF	AU	BU	GEM
10%	10%	10%	15%	20%	15%	10%	10%

10% STRUCK WITH FULL HEADS

This coin has a sharp, thinner date, somewhat modified from previous years. Some specimens of this date have a very porous field. The date may have been modified in 1923.

The date on this coin was thinned and tapered by at least 50% in an attempt to give the dies better wearing qualities and striking abilities. This thinner date was the type of date that was used when the date was recessed in 1925. Most compare this date with the 1925, 1926 and 1927, etc., or most Philadelphia mints in 1920's. But not so. It should be more closely compared with the 1923 mintage; it is relatively close. However the 1924-P is much more available in FH than the 1923-P which has proven to be very scarce in Full Head. Most Full Heads command two to three times Guidebook prices.

GRADING:

OBVERSE

Normally a strong strike for pre-'25's. Many variations of color in this date and mintmark; but still Uncirculated. Shield usually strong also. Should grade on upper end of scale.

REVERSE

Stronger than normal-especially in the center of the breast and along the front edge of the eagle's wings.

NOTE: I have just examined a 1924 that at first glance appears to be a "specimen" coin or Matte Proof. However, since there are no mint records on either you must assume that it is a first strike from a new die. Also since the horizontal lines in the shield are not struck up and the vertical lines are not that sharp (compared with the known 1916-1917 Matte Proof) you must come to the same conclusion. But compared with other 1924-P it sure is a premium strike. The toes also are mushy and struck weak and the reed and bead on the obverse is somewhat flat on top ridges from about 3 o'clock to 6 o'clock, which is not a characteristic on matte proof or specimen coins. However the hair and FH is so superb you can count the strands of hair above her temple and on the back of her head.

* * *

AVAILABILITY OF FULL HEADS:

		MS64	MS65	MS66	MS67
FULL HEADS:	PCGS	30	10	4	3
	NGC	29	12	1	1
NON-FULL HEADS:					
	PCGS	83	7	4	4
	NGC	48	18	5	4

All of the high-end pieces in this date and mintmark seem to come from the same die. Some would call it a "rusty" die or matte finish die, as it produces a near-matte finish coin. With nearly eleven million pieces struck, I don't think the dies had time to rust.

Of the three P.C.G.S. MS67 FH's - I disagree with one piece. I saw the piece when it was in an MS66 FH holder. I don't agree with the upgrade because it was a bit too bagmarked to warrant the MS67 FH. This is just one man's opinion, however. I have placed four of the other P.C.G.S. pieces and three of the N.G.C. pieces, and agreed with the full head on all of them.

1924-D

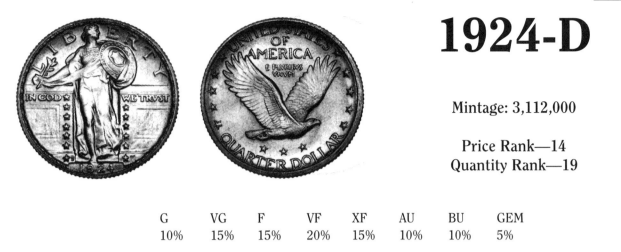

G	VG	F	VF	XF	AU	BU	GEM
10%	15%	15%	20%	15%	10%	10%	5%

LESS THAN 10% OR LESS STRUCK WITH FULL HEADS

The 1924-D is a bit more scarce than once thought in MS 65FH and better. PCGS has encapsulated 22 in MS 65FH and 5 pieces in MS66FH with none higher. NGC has 12 pieces in MS 65FH and 4 in MS 66FH with none higher. In my first revision, price ranked it 15th; presently it is ranked 13th in price rarity.

Many specimens of this date and mintmark come weakly struck, particularly around the date and rivets on the shield. This says nothing about the characteristically weak head. There are some screamers out there in MS 65FH and MS 66FH with strong dates, but it takes a lot of shoe leather to find them! Many have the top 1/3 or 1/2 of the date missing from wear or from a broken die. There are many varieties with broken dies through the date, so when the die broke, the Mint apparently kept striking them. Then the die continued to crumble and finally break away completely resulting in the missing 1/3 to 1/2 of the date on many 1924-D's.

Fairly common in uncirculated condition without a full head. Total pieces encapsulated by PCGS at this writing including all MS FH and non-FH's is 1,012. At NGC the number for all is 528 pieces.

A very strange paradox regarding this date and mintmark. Many show up in high circulated grades, but not many in G/VG/F. With the 1924-S the opposite is true.

GRADING:

OBVERSE

Most always struck weakly. Die breaks all around date. Top half of date weak or missing altogether. Many with lots of smaller bagmarks, obverse and reverse. Several rivets missing from shield. Head is frequently incused or dished in similar to the classic Flat Head; the 1926-D.

REVERSE

Usually weak, also. Especially eagle's breast and left wing.

* * *

AVAILABILITY OF FULL HEADS:

		MS65	MS66	MS67
FULL HEADS:	PCGS	22	5	0
	NGC	12	4	0
NON-FULL HEADS:				
	PCGS	264	26	2
	NGC	155	67	19

There are several encapsulated 1924-D's in MS65 FH and MS66 FH that have the top half of the date missing. I believe this grade is too high and should have been assigned MS64 FH. I truly believe this weakness of date should be reflected in the grade and in my opinion an MS65 or MS66 cannot have this weakness.

The MS66 FH's that remain (both N.G.C. and P.C.G.S. holders) have complete dates. The auction of the Museum of Connecticut History's holdings held by Heritage June 1-3, 1995 was accompanied by a rumor that there were two rolls of 1924-D's. The rumor stated that most of the pieces were MS66 non-full head, but fifteen or sixteen pieces were MS67. These pieces auctioned in Long Beach, California in one session and this large offering of so many pieces of one date and mintmark at one time was detrimental to this segment of the series for quite some time.

There are many die breaks at and around the date on this particular date of Standing Liberty Quarter.

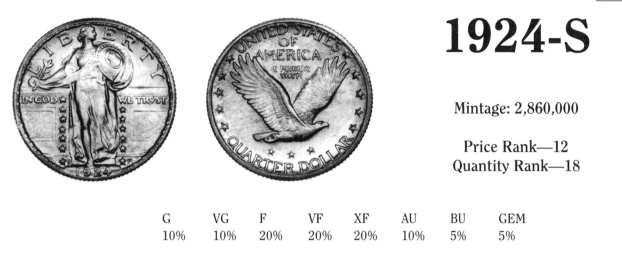

1924-S

Mintage: 2,860,000

Price Rank—12
Quantity Rank—18

G	VG	F	VF	XF	AU	BU	GEM
10%	10%	20%	20%	20%	10%	5%	5%

2% OR LESS STRUCK WITH FULL HEADS

Some modification on the shield and rivets; and the date is also much thinner. Again, perhaps there were some modifications of the "S" mint in 1924 as was the case with the Philadelphia mint. This explains why this date is usually strong, yet the rest of the coin is very weak (as was the 1924-S dollar and the 1924-S cent). This seemed to be an era when San Francisco was having more than normal striking problems.

There is a re-punched mintmark of this date that appears as though three "3" 's have been put together, each on top of the other. However, I think this was done outside of the Mint as the S mint marks seem as though they are the strongest part of the coin and are not uniform with the rest of the coin for wear.

Very scarce in sharp Full Head and worth five to ten times flathead in this condition. Therefore, due consideration should be given when grading most grades of this date. (When your author makes the above statement about the grading, "circulated" means the top grades-VF and up.)

High grades are missing from the bourse floors-low grades are dominant. Just the opposite of the sister coin (1924-D).

GRADING:

As with most "S" mints, weakly struck.

OBVERSE
Head and shield weak. Just a little wear makes the coin appear as one to two grades less.

REVERSE
Normal weakness on reverse "S" mints does prevail. Eagle's breast feathers are softly struck or "mushed" together.

* * *

AVAILABILITY OF FULL HEADS:

		MS65	MS66	MS67
FULL HEADS:	PCGS	10	3	0
	NGC	8	2	0
NON-FULL HEADS:				
	PCGS	18	7	1
	NGC	25	12	2

Wow! Nearly three million pieces minted and only twenty-three pieces in MS65 FH and MS66 FH combined. I have handled both N.G.C. MS 66 FH's, and each was nice. Two pieces of the P.C.G.S. MS66 FH were clearly not FH's in my opinion. Again, must be the early grading? They just would not "cut the mustard" in today's stricter grading. Approximately half do not quite make it because the line at and below her ear is very faint or nonexistent. There is a piece in a P.C.G.S. holder that is graded MS66 that should be designated full head, but is not. Many people have submitted this one for full head, but P.C.G.S. has not agreed at this point in time.

The piece that was sold in The Boys Town Sale by Superior in 1990 lacked a full 20% of being full head, but was in an MS66 FH holder. The second MS66 FH has a bad mark in the hairline area and some would argue that it should not even be called full head. The Boys Town piece opened at $10,000 and ultimately sold for $14,000 plus the 10% buyer's fee. This without a strong full head. WOW!

1925

Mintage: 12,280,000

Price Rank—34
Quantity Rank—35

G	VG	F	VF	XF	AU	BU	GEM
10%	15%	25%	15%	20%	5%	5%	5%

5% STRUCK WITH FULL HEADS

TYPE III, RECESSED DATE.

The high relief date positioned on the first step of the passway proved to have very poor wear qualities, so in 1925 the entire area of the first step was incused or recessed to receive the date. Hence, the date wore with the coin and lasted much, much longer. Until this time, a coin may be as good as very fine with almost no date. The 1925 Philadelphia mintmark in Full Head is about as available as the 1927-P in F.H., tougher than the 1929-P and 1930-P, but more available than the 1926-P and 1928-P. Frequently available in CH.BU., M.S. 65/66 Full Head.

Rating the "P" mints from 1925 to 1930 in rarity:

1925 4th
1926 2nd
1927 3rd
1928 1st
1929 5th
1930 6th

GRADING:

OBVERSE

First year for recessed date. Not usually strongly struck. Full detail, but soft lines in shield (vertical and horizontal)- usually missing or very weak.

REVERSE

At least an average strike on eagle's breast feathers. Can come strongly struck with a little bit of looking.

* * *

AVAILABILITY OF FULL HEADS:

		MS65	MS66	MS67
FULL HEADS:	PCGS	59	13	3
	NGC	17	5	3
NON-FULL HEADS:				
	PCGS	66	7	0
	NGC	28	0	0

There seems to be an adequate supply of the 1925 in MS65 FH, MS66 FH, and MS67 FH. Of the pieces I have placed, perhaps as many as one half of them have a weakness at her temple. This, as is the case of many other encapsulated pieces, probably would not grade a "full head" in today's grading. I believe as many as 25% just would not make the grade today.

This is one of the dates where I think there have been MANY broken out to resubmit, but the tabs or inserts were not returned to the grading services. I question the high number of full head pieces. There are no MS67 non-full heads. WHY! It is a strange dilemma. With the mintage over twelve million pieces, some of us wonder why there aren't some quality pieces in non-full head. Even the piece in the Smithsonian collection is a circulated piece. Perhaps there is a surprise or two out there for some fortunate collector who will stumble upon a few pieces. Maybe even a roll of them. Ha-Ha!

1926

Mintage: 11,316,000

Price Rank—24
Quantity Rank—32

G	VG	F	VF	XF	AU	BU	GEM
10%	15%	15%	15%	20%	15%	5%	5%

10% STRUCK WITH FULL HEADS

The 1926, for some strange reason, is usually as weak a strike as most "S" mints and most Full Heads are much more rare than most people realize. A Full Head is well worth three to five times Guidebook prices.

There are a few broken dies of this year, giving Miss Liberty the appearance of another fold in her gown at her left leg. For you die variety collectors, I have heard and seen very few of these in the 35 years I have collected Standing Liberty Quarters.

GRADING:

OBVERSE
Usually well to above average strike. Can expect this date and mintmark to grade high on grading scale. Should meet all requirements for Ty. 111 Standing Liberty Quarters.

REVERSE
Usually as well struck as the obverse. Above average strike here as well.

*   *   *

AVAILABILITY OF FULL HEADS:

		MS65	MS66	MS67
FULL HEADS:	PCGS	28	2	0
	NGC	15	1	0
NON-FULL HEADS:				
	PCGS	72	10	1
	NGC	32	0	1

This date seems to be a sleeper - only forty-six pieces total in MS65 FH and MS66 FH combined. There is one collector we know who likes to accumulate this date, but only chooses about one in three pieces for one reason or another. Many of these are weak at the temple. When searching for the ultimate full head, even in MS65 FH they are hard to find - especially the bright one.

Compared to the 1926: the 1925 has more than twice the number of pieces that 1926 has in full head.

I think one of the 1926's in MS66 FH was the piece that was auctioned in 1990 in The Boys Town Sale by Superior, and in 1994 in the Rothenberger sale. I purchased it in 1994 and placed it immediately. Since that time, one other MS66 FH has been encapsulated by P.C.G.S. I also placed the lone N.G.C. MS66 FH piece which has a sharp full head, and is bright white. At this time, only three pieces are encapsulated in MS66 FH, both services.

1926-D

Mintage: 1,716,000

Price Rank—4
Quantity Rank—10

G	VG	F	VF	XF	AU	BU	GEM
13%	15%	20%	15%	10%	10%	15%	2%

1% or LESS STRUCK WITH FULL HEADS

There are many specimens with die breaks starting with a dot on the edge extending through the word "Liberty". This coin has been listed as scarce in some past numismatic publication ads, and this is true only if you are collecting by die varieties. The 1926-D is the classic in two categories: most available and most flat heads. The mintage figures do seem too low for this date considering their availability. The second classic aspect of this date is-it almost never comes with a full head. True full heads are worth at least ten times Guidebook prices. The ratio of Full Heads versus flat heads is about 100 to 1.

A true Full Head on a 1926-D in MS 65/66 is easily a $30/$45,000 coin and that is for today's price. An original roll surfaced in the Midwest in 1984 and not a single piece was a Full Head. (I bought several that were called "virtually a Full Head". HA! HA!) The flat head in this year is common knowledge in the numismatic world. Most collectors and dealers are aware of this fact.

GRADING:

OBVERSE

Almost never a Full Head. The classic flat head of the series. Usually incused in head. Little, if any, design in shield and many rivets missing.

REVERSE

Frequently weak strike. Few, if any, feathers on eagle's wings; so with just a touch of wear, this coin will appear at least one or two grades lower.

* * *

AVAILABILITY OF FULL HEADS:

		MS64	MS65	MS66	MS67
FULL HEADS:	PCGS	11	7	2	0
	NGC	12	3	0	0
NON-FULL HEADS:					
	PCGS	681	62	2	0
	NGC	304	60	0	0

The Boys Town Sale, 5/90 Superior, did not have a FH piece. The two MS66 FH that exist are as follows. The first piece is shimmering white, sharp full head, and we had it encapsulated. The second piece is from the Rothenberger sale, 1/94. I bought and placed this piece, but it is inferior to the first piece. The second was one of the MS65 FH pieces that upgraded, but in my opinion should not have done so. Recently placed the NGC piece; light golden and light russet around the periphery with a sharp full head. A very high-end piece for and MS65 FH.

Even if you include the MS64 FH's this date is still extremely rare and commands about 1/2 the price of an MS65 FH for the MS64 FH. PCGS has slabbed 7 in MS64 FH and NGC has slabbed 6 pieces. How many were extra tries for a higher grade?

I personally know a dealer who kept trying for the first 1926-D MS66 FH. He submitted the same coin over and over and kept getting the MS65 FH grade. He kept the inserts and the population at PCGS grew to 11 pieces. I encouraged him to turn in the inserts from the break-outs and when he did the number of MS65 FH 1926-D's at PCGS dropped from 11 pieces to 5 pieces. I guess he kept all of them and sent all of them in. The figure is now 6 pieces in MS65 FH and 2 pieces in MS66 FH at PCGS and only eleven pieces in MS64 FH. NGC has none higher than in MS65 FH, and there are only three in MS65 FH! Extremely rare in full head. Even AU full head, this piece will fetch serious money.

1926-S

Mintage: 2,700,000

Price Rank—6
Quantity Rank—17

G	VG	F	VF	XF	AU	BU	GEM
20%	27%	10%	10%	15%	10%	5%	3%

1% OR LESS STRUCK WITH FULL HEADS

The 1926-S is like all "S" mints in the twenties. San Francisco had many problems striking any coins up to par with the other minting facilities. Brown & Dunn grading makes certain consideration when grading most 1920 "S" mint coins, and this is especially true of the Standing Liberty Quarters. The 1926-S or 1927-S are the most weakly struck of all "S" mints in the twenties. The mintage figure of this date seems a bit high, also. A true Full Head, M.S. 65/65 would closely compare in value to the 1916. A much underrated coin, if not THE underrated coin of the entire series, except for the 1920-S and 1926-D in Full Head.

I have probably handled 150+ coins (or so) of this date and mintmark since my book was issued originally in 1976. The number of known true Full Heads MS encapsulated would number 15 pieces or less. During that time, I have attended most major auctions and conventions in the United States. In reality, the 1926-S should be much closer to the 1927-S Full Head in price. It is nearly as scarce. A close second.

Teardrop 1926-S, Contributed by my friends, Aram and Nancy Haroutunian. Extra metal beside Miss Liberty's leg in the shape of a teardrop. To the author's knowledge, the highest grade that has surfaced is an MS62 coin. Are there higher grades? A very unusual Standing Liberty Quarter cud.

In the last few years, I have come to know Aram Haroutunian and his lovely wife, Nancy, from the Los Angeles, California area. He brought to my attention (and gave me one piece) a coin that has an extra drop of metal by the side of Miss Liberty's left leg. It is in the shape of a teardrop, and is so named by this gentleman. It is interesting that this coin cannot be found in high grades. I have seen the coin in AU and MS 62, having owned two in AU and one encapsulated MS 62. Neither PCGS nor NGC identifies this as a teardrop on the holder. Could this be changed??

Take a close look at your 1926-S's and see if you are the lucky individual that has a high grade with this interesting addition of metal by Miss Liberty's leg.

GRADING:

OBVERSE
Usually compares most favorably with the 1927-S as far as strike is concerned. Most always weak-especially head and shield, as well as the rivets on the inner shield. Keep this weakness in mind when grading this date and mint-mark.

REVERSE
Most always weak in eagle's breast, but very lustrous.

AVAILABILITY OF FULL HEADS:

		MS64	MS65	MS66	MS67
FULL HEADS:	PCGS	5	5	1	0
	NGC	5	7	0	0
NON-FULL HEADS:					
	PCGS	37	6	0	
	NGC	14	0	0	

The lone MS66 FH piece (PCGS) is a sharp FH and deserves the grade in my opinion. There are only two bag marks on the entire coin - one on Miss Liberty's left thigh and a light scratch on the reverse under the eagle's wing. On even the finest 1926-S's out there, the 3rd and 4th rivets are missing from the outer shield. Keep this in mind when you look at all grades of 1926-S. I have placed 5 of the NGC MS65 FH's and these pieces are about the bottom/lower end regarding the requirements for FH. Have also placed 3 of PCGS pieces in MS65 FH, which had a bit stronger heads - but not by much. If you consider the MS64 FH's at both services, you still only add 10 pieces to the availability. I am reasonably sure several of these MS64 FH's have been submitted more than once and I think some of the inserts are yet to be sent back to have them removed from the population reports.

1927

Mintage: 11,912,000

Price Rank—33
Quantity Rank—34

G	VG	F	VF	XF	AU	BU	GEM
10%	10%	10%	10%	15%	20%	10%	15%

ABOUT 10% STRUCK WITH FULL HEADS

The 1927 is among the most available and one of the most common in Full Head, though not quite as common as the 1930. It is rated thirty-fourth in mintage and price-wise rates as thirty-second. As you can see, it is about in its right category. Having said "common", your author would again like to clear a point. NO Standing Liberty Quarter in Full Head is common. That statement is made in comparison with other Standing Liberty Quarters with Full Heads.

Frequently used as Ty. II and Ty. III for type, as it can be had very readily with a Full Head. Many flashy coins of this date exist. Beautifully brilliant and blast white.

The higher the mintage, the more new dies that are used, and consequently more Full Heads. This seems to be true of this date and mintmark also. But it is not consistent throughout the entire Standing Liberty Quarter series.

GRADING:

OBVERSE

One of the strongest strikes after 1925-the strongest being 1929 and 1930. Expect this "P" mint to grade toward the top of the grading scale.

REVERSE

Usually strong strike as well. Especially the breast feathers on the eagle and his wing feathers, too. Many pin feathers (the shorter feathers) pronounced as well.

* * *

AVAILABILITY OF FULL HEADS:

		MS65	MS66	MS67
FULL HEADS:	PCGS	46	7	0
	NGC	16	2	0
NON-FULL HEADS:				
	PCGS	44	7	1
	NGC	28	6	0

Quite a bit can be said about this nonpretentious date. With a mintage of nearly 12 million, you would expect more than 71 pieces to grade MS65 FH and MS66 FH! (There is one in MS67 at this writing at PCGS.) I placed one of the NGC MS66 FH's - and she's a beauty! Light peripheral toning; light to medium golden well-matched toning on obverse and reverse, with a sharp full head! I have gotten encapsulated and placed 5 of the PCGS pieces in MS66 FH, as well as many of the MS65 FH's in both NGC and PCGS holders. There are some from both services that would not fall into the sharp full head category required in today's grading. I also think this is another of those "common date" MS65 FH dates where some are sent in more than once, thereby inflating the figures in the population reports. Many tabs/inserts were not returned to the grading services when the practice of breaking out coins to resubmit them for a higher grade began.

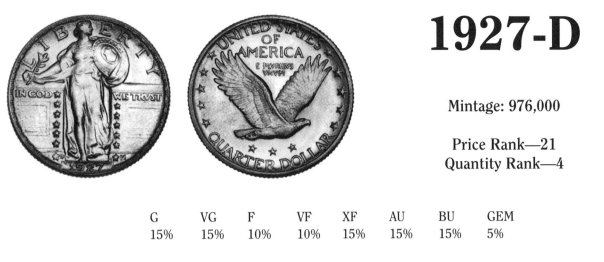

1927-D

Mintage: 976,000

Price Rank—21
Quantity Rank—4

G	VG	F	VF	XF	AU	BU	GEM
15%	15%	10%	10%	15%	15%	15%	5%

3% STRUCK WITH FULL HEADS

The 1927-D is commonly a weak strike. It is also not readily available with a Full Head.

This is one of those dates upon which your author would challenge the "reported" mintage figures. If there were a way of making available the daily work sheet posted on each press with its daily run, I think you would find a conflict. This date is found at least ten to twenty-five times more frequently than its sister coin, the 1927-S; yet the reported mintage is not even three times as great and is usually in uncirculated condition (though most of those are flat heads). Using a mathematical break-down in comparing it with the 1927-S, your author would estimate the mintage to be more in the three million range (or more). This is another one of those sleepers in the series, if indeed the mintage figures are correct. As you can see, quantity puts it close to the top, in fourth position. Frequently last stars on bottom are flat.

GRADING:

OBVERSE

Most always poor to medium strike. Especially head and lines on shield, both vertical and horizontal. Most of the time the 3rd and 4th rivets are missing from the shield as well.

REVERSE

Most always weak-especially in the center of the eagle's breast.

* * *

AVAILABILITY OF FULL HEADS:

		MS65	MS66	MS67
FULL HEADS:	PCGS	28	3	0
	NGC	5	2	0
NON-FULL HEADS:				
	PCGS	105	4	0
	NGC	56	0	3

The lone NGC piece is a real screamer Sharp Full Head! Lovely toning around the periphery. An outstanding coin! One of the MS66 FH's sold in the Rothenberger sale, 1/94 Superior. Head was weaker than the NGC piece and had almost no shield lines visible. Also, a sizable bag scrape on Miss Liberty's left leg. I felt it was a low-end MS66 FH; bought it and placed it.

The other MS66 FH lives out West and the N.G.C. piece is the finest in my opinion of the three pieces encapsulated. Coin is white with a sharp full head and toes. This is the second P.C.G.S. piece. I have purchased and placed many of the MS65 FH's. Of those twenty-eight pieces at least twenty have come through this office. As I have mentioned before, I do not always agree with the grading services on the full head description. The 1927-D has a tendency to be a bit weak in the temple area. So pick and choose. I DO!

The finest 1927-D I've seen lives in the Smithsonian Institute in their collection of United States Numismatics. I believe this coin would grade MS67-68 FH. Prooflike reverse and somewhat prooflike obverse, although not as apparent as the reverse.

1927-S

Mintage: 396,000

Price Rank—2
Quantity Rank—3

G	VG	F	VF	XF	AU	BU	GEM
10%	17%	10%	30%	20%	5%	5%	3%

LESS THAN 1% STRUCK WITH FULL HEADS

A word of caution concerning this date. There are many with added mintmarks. The added mintmarks are usually easy to detect, as the "S" is usually "blobbed", or tilted, or off-location. Also, the most detectable is: the bottom half of the "S" mintmark looks like 3/4 of a circle on the non-genuine pieces. The genuine "S" mintmark is equal-top and bottom. This was added to the P-mint which in itself is struck differently than the S-mint. P-mint coins are usually strong in the head and rivets on shield, details almost not at all found on the 1927-S. Instead, many pieces of the 1927-S are weakly struck overall, although very bright. They are extremely weak in the torso, but flat with only 70-80% of the detail. The reverse will be very weak, also. There are also many pieces that are cast. Look for granular surfaces and a railroad rim (doubled). Frequently, the outer wings on eagle on reverse will be strong.

The 1927-S has such a low mintage that the existence of Full Heads is few. If all Full Heads had been kept from getting into circulation, it would still have been the scarcest "S" mint of the entire series, excluding the 1918/7-S. Your author is giving it a liberal 1% struck with Full Heads. That would make it about 3,900 that were available with Full Heads if all were kept. This figure is considerably less than the above estimate because some, indeed, did make it into circulation. Your author would rate it three to five times more rare than the 1916 in Full Head, though the present price is not in line with the real scarcity of the coin. In the 40 years your author has collected and admired these coins, the ratio has been at least one to twenty-five in relation to the 1916 with Full Heads.

*Author's note: Why is the 1923-S almost four times the mintage-yet the 1923-S is about ten times the price in low grades. WHY?? Why are both coins struck at the same mint in the same era, yet the 1923-S is many times more valuable than the 1927-S in lower circulated grades? Why?

GRADING:

OBVERSE
Like most "S" mint coins, this date comes weakly struck. Very weak, especially in the head, shield, lines on shield (vertical and horizontal). Full Heads in uncirculated condition are almost nonexistent. Do not look for much head, even in CH.BU, M.S. 65/65. Almost nonexistent.

REVERSE
Most always weak breast feathers. Sometimes outer wings will be strong.

* * *

AVAILABILITY OF FULL HEADS:

		MS64	MS65	MS66	MS67
FULL HEADS:	PCGS	2	0	1	0
	NGC	3	1	0	0
NON-FULL HEADS:					
	PCGS	29	20	11	2
	NGC	14	8	9	0

Enough cannot be said about the 1927-S in full head. It is as scarce as the overdate with a full head. If you count the MS64 FH's along with the MS65 FH and the MS66 FH, there are only seven pieces. I have had encapsulated and/or placed five of those seven pieces. One of the MS64 FH pieces did not receive the full head designation the first time through the grading service. The MS66 FH is a bit weak in the forehead area and the ear is nearly always weak on the rest of these. The N.G.C. MS65 FH is a close second to the P.C.G.S. MS66 FH. Both coins have just a kiss of light golden toning. The weakness in the ear area is an accepted factor on the 1927-S. The other MS64 FH pieces are weak in this area also, as are all of the pieces a bit weak.

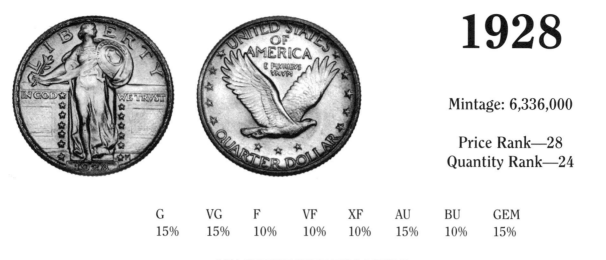

1928

Mintage: 6,336,000

Price Rank—28
Quantity Rank—24

G	VG	F	VF	XF	AU	BU	GEM
15%	15%	10%	10%	10%	15%	10%	15%

20% STRUCK WITH FULL HEADS

The 1928, like the 1927, is among the most common and most available. Unlike its sister coin (1927), the number of mintage puts it twenty-fourth and the price puts it twenty-eighth. It is somewhat underrated because it is nearly six million less than the 1927.

The higher the mintage, more dies are used; hence, more Full Heads. But, of course, this is not always true. The reverse of the above statement is often true. The old, worn dies are used far beyond their normal expected life and, as a result, the largest mintage is also the most flat heads. So, on a direct ratio basis, there should be about half as many Full Heads of this date as there are of 1927.

Overall, struck a little better than average, though a Full Head still commands a substantial premium over an average uncirculated coin (M.S. 60 with a flat head).

GRADING:

Frequently comes with an excellent Full Head and with much eye appeal that is fully brilliant.

OBVERSE

Most of this date and mintmark come strongly struck: Liberty's gown, head, shield and toes should all meet normal grading criteria.

REVERSE

Usually well struck, as are most "P" mints from 1925-1930. Sharp breast feathers as well as edges of eagle's wings. Many coins of this date and mintmark will please the most exacting connoisseur of the Standing Liberty Quarter series.

* * *

AVAILABILITY OF FULL HEADS:

		MS65	MS66	MS67	MS68
FULL HEADS:	PCGS	29	8	1	0
	NGC	17	4	0	0
NON-FULL HEADS:					
	PCGS	36	6	0	0
	NGC	38	27	9	0

Generally referred to as a "common" date. With only 59 pieces encapsulated in MS65 FH, MS66 FH and MS67 FH, total, you certainly cannot call it common! Only thirteen pieces are MS66 FH and MS67 FH both services combined. WOW!! An entire roll of these was offered to me by another dealer at the A.N.A. convention in Orlando in 1992. All forty pieces were encapsulated by N.G.C. and all pieces were very colorful; medium golden/rose and light russet. Many pieces were graded MS66 non-full head (hence the high number encapsulated by N.G.C.) He offered the forty-piece roll to me at $44,000, but I declined. Later the roll sold for $36,000 to another dealer, and then I purchased the pieces I wanted from him. I have seen several colorful MS66 pieces in P.C.G.S. holders since that time, and some of the MS66 FH pieces in P.C.G.S. holders are also colorful, so perhaps they were crossed over the N.G.C. holders. I have placed two of the N.G.C. MS66 FH's and four of the P.C.G.S. MS66 FH's. All were excellent strikes with sharp full heads.

The lone P.C.G.S. MS67 FH was offered in the Rothenberger sale (1/94 Superior) where it realized $7,000 plus the 10% buyer's fee. As I viewed the auction lots, I took notes as follows: "Sharp full head. Vertical lines, but no horizontal lines. Tone: rose and satiny". This is the same piece that sold in The Boys Town Sale (Superior, 1990) for $15,000 plus the 10%. I was winning bidder at that sale for that piece, but the set was sold as an intact lot, #3756. So..... we all lost the pieces we had "won" in bids throughout the sale of the set.

1928-D

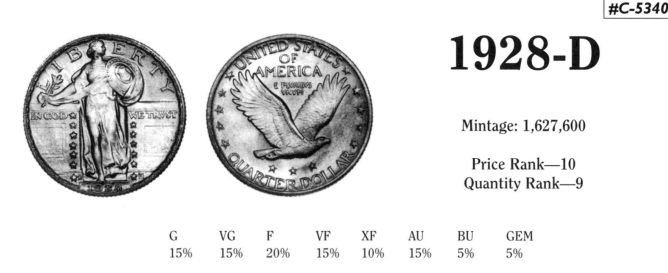

Mintage: 1,627,600

Price Rank—10
Quantity Rank—9

G	VG	F	VF	XF	AU	BU	GEM
15%	15%	20%	15%	10%	15%	5%	5%

1% OR LESS STRUCK WITH FULL HEADS

The 1928-D, when compared to the 1919-S, has 109,000 less mintage. Since the 1919-S is considered a key date, you can readily see that the 1928-D should be considered somewhere near a key or semi-key date. This is not so; it is one of the most available in uncirculated condition, M.S. 60 with a <u>flat head</u>. This is another date on which many question the total mintage reports. It does seem low for the number of this date that are actually available today. In Full Head, the M.S. 65 + is a much sought-after coin and not readily available.

Full Heads of this date are easily worth more than 10 times flat head prices, or even more if the piece is outstanding. Full mint bloom of this date and mintmark could easily demand $7,900 +.

GRADING:

OBVERSE

Usually soft or "mushy" strike. Detail is there, but weak. Shield frequently lacks in detail, especially the lines on the inner shield.

REVERSE

Usually weak to very weak, especially in center of eagle's breast feathers and the feather on the edge of the left wing.

*　*　*

AVAILABILITY OF FULL HEADS:

		MS64	MS65	MS66	MS67
FULL HEADS:	PCGS	20	9	7	0
	NGC	16	12	2	0
NON-FULL HEADS:					
	PCGS	310	20	1	
	NGC	133	14	0	

Lot # 1380 in the 1/94 Superior Auction Galleries' Rothenberger sale was not a high-end piece and just barely made the grade assigned, in my opinion. It had a large bag mark on her neck! I have placed many other of the MS65 FH and MS66 FH pieces from both major services, but about 25% of the pieces I have seen were not pieces I would place, as I did not agree they were full head specimens. Most 1928-D's in high grade are white like the 1926-D's but many are weak in the temple area. A much underrated coin in today's market.

What a great way to control a single date and mintmark and only purchase sixty-six coins to do so! I guess someone might make some serious money doing that? I am including the MS64 FH pieces which make up about 60% of the total MS FH pieces. Think about it.

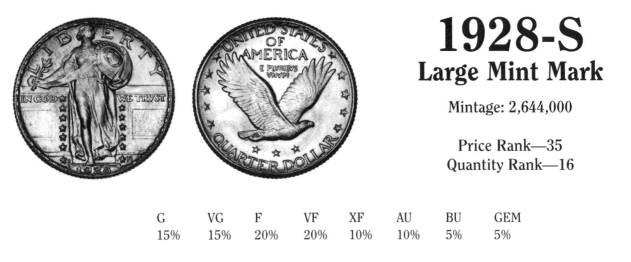

1928-S
Large Mint Mark

Mintage: 2,644,000

Price Rank—35
Quantity Rank—16

G	VG	F	VF	XF	AU	BU	GEM
15%	15%	20%	20%	10%	10%	5%	5%

5% OR LESS STRUCK WITH FULL HEADS

The 1928-S is another of the "S" mints which is somewhat tough in Full Head in the 1920's.

The large and small mintmark of this year do exist, and the small mintmark is three to five times more rare than the large mintmark. There is a similarity in appearance, as with the 1945-S, micro "S" Mercury Dime. It is easily discernible- especially in a side-by-side comparison. Once in a while, these mintmarks are put on at the mother mint and when they are, they are usually much smaller. Another explanation is that the mint workers who install the new dies have a punch-like tool with that particular mintmark which they put on when the new die is installed. Since these punches are not furnished by the mint, but each employee is responsible for his own tools, you could possibly come up with several sizes of mintmarks in any given year. i.e. the 1960-D Lincoln Cent. On the large mintmark, the "S" touches the last star on the left.

GRADING:

OBVERSE

Look for weakness in Miss Liberty's temple. Olive leaves in Miss Liberty's hair are frequently flat. *Note: Temple area frequently comes weak. Looks full, but!!! LOOK AGAIN. The full line separating Miss Liberty's temple and hairline may not be distinct.

REVERSE

Medium to poor, though not as weak as the 1927-S. Look for some weakness in the breast feathers.

* * *

#C-5358. The shooting star variety. The only one to date that has been discovered. (A very interesting die break-away and the end result is an interesting cud or "shooting star: variety.

AVAILABILITY OF FULL HEADS:

		MS65	MS66	MS67
FULL HEADS:	PCGS	69	21	2
	NGC	54	10	2
NON-FULL HEADS:				
	PCGS	248	38	0
	NGC	135	33	2

I have placed one of the N.G.C. and one of the P.C.G.S. MS67 FH's. Each was medium to heavily toned, but had great full heads! I crossed the first P.C.G.S. piece to N.G.C. at my customer's request, and since the grading service did not return the insert to me, there may be only one piece at N.G.C. and one at P.C.G.S.?

Such a common date coin, yet very elusive in MS66 FH and MS67 FH. Only 35 pieces total in the two services and that number would only be correct if all inserts/tabs have been returned to the grading services after break-outs for resubmission.

#C-5351

1928-s
Small Mint Mark

Mintage: Unknown

G	VG	F	VF	XF	AU	BU	GEM
15%	15%	20%	20%	10%	10%	5%	5%

5% OR LESS STRUCK WITH FULL HEADS

The small mintmark is further to the right and down toward the date and does not touch the star. It is more rare than the large mintmark and has probably gone unnoticed by most collectors until about 10 years ago. This variety was added to the Guidebook in 1976. Some varieties have the mintmark setting below the point of the star.

There seem to be only one or two dies of the small mintmark of this date.

GRADING:

OVERALL
Can come very well struck, but usually not. Take your time in selecting this Standing Liberty Quarter. Your rewards will be worth it. Overall a better strike than the "S" large mintmark.

Repunched Mintmarks of 1928

Mintage: UNKNOWN
Price Rank N/A
Quantity Rank N/A

There are four major repunched mintmarks for 1928. I have listed them below:

1928-D/D: (#C-5342) The 1928 D/D always shows broken dies at Miss Liberty's toes, all the way across the "D" and through the bottom star. There is a lesser die break in the edge of Miss Liberty's gown.

1928-D/S (#C-5345) The S passes through the center of "D" and with a 10x loupe it is usually very discernible. Also, above the "D".

1928-S/S (large S / small s) (#C-5356) Most of the bottom serif of the "S" shows below the other "S". Usually very distinct, even without magnification.

1928-S/D (#C-5357) A bit hard to distinguish but with a 10x or more can tell it very well, though it looks like a blobbed "D". So look carefully at this one.

As with most of our U.S. coinage, there exists in virtually every series some retooling-overdates-one mintmark over the other- double dates-double struck-hub doubling, and blunt or pointed dates and letters-off-metals. Some make it in books or plastic boards- some do not. Remember the 1964 Roosevelt Dime (pointed tail on 9)?? Or, the 1970 cud Lincoln Cent??? Very popular in their day. But, now popularity is diminished.

There are five such in the Standing Liberty Quarter series; 1928-S/ S, 1928-D/S, 1928-D/D, 1928-S/D as well as the 1924-S triple punched mintmark. These seem very popular with Standing Liberty Quarter enthusiasts-but this enthusiasm is not always shared with the rest of the numismatic world. They are, indeed, done at the U.S. Mint, and planned. NO ACCIDENT. Your author's opinion is: any- coin that is re-engraved, over-mintmarked, overdated, or otherwise planned by minting officials should be included in building a set.

The over mintmark is usually the result of the die installer or job setter punching in the mintmark when he installs the new die. Sometimes, not happy with the results, he hits it again. D/S is the result of one die prepared at one branch mint but shipped and used at a different branch mint. Sometimes the mintmark is already on the new die coming from the mother mint.

As far as true scarcity is concerned, the mintage would only be a few thousand compared with the regular mintage and should be worth many times more. Because the over-mintmark is not popular with all collectors, demand is much less. Hence, value is about the same as a regular mintmark or slightly more- maybe as much as l/2 to 2 times more. There is very little to go on except the formula above. Buyer vs Seller-Seller vs Buyer. Nothing in print. It is like trading horses. Whatever two people are comfortable with. All in all, adding the over-mintmark is adding spice to collecting, which is why we collect in the beginning. I think you should add all or some to your collection of Standing Liberty Quarters.

1928-S/D

1928-D/D. Note the toes on this coin have been re-worked.

1928-D/D

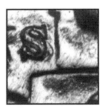

1928-S/S
Large S/tilted S

1928-S/S
Large S/S

1929

Mintage: 11,140,000

Price Rank—36
Quantity Rank—31

G	VG	F	VF	XF	AU	BU	GEM
10%	10%	10%	10%	10%	15%	15%	20%

50% STRUCK WITH FULL HEADS

The 1929 is closely paralleled to the 1930, which is the most "common" of all Standing Liberty Quarters. The 1929 is second most common in Full Head, with at least 50 percent struck originally with Full Heads. Percentages are deceiving, however, because in actual numbers there are much fewer than the 1930. For the 1929, there are only 156 in MS65FH and 22 in MS66/67FH, both services, so a total of 178. But the number of MS 65/66/67FH for 1930 is a whopping 557 pieces. It is not as close as once thought. It is a very distant second.

With price this date is rated thirty-seventh and in quantity it is rated thirty-first. This indicates the accuracy and the necessity of a price/quantity analysis.

GRADING:

OBVERSE
Above normal strike. Frequently comes fully brilliant or satiny white. Beautiful cartwheel effect can be obtained. Be selective. Should grade high on the scale. Struck just about as strongly as the 1930-P.

REVERSE
Usually nice strike. Full feathers on the eagle and a bold strike as well. Should meet all grading criteria for Standing Liberty Quarters.

* * *

AVAILABILITY OF FULL HEADS:

		MS65	MS66	MS67	MS68
FULL HEADS:	PCGS	137	17	0	0
	NGC	46	6	1	0
NON-FULL HEADS:					
	PCGS	68	12	0	0
	NGC	28	6	1	0

Wow and wow! What happened here? Only 24 pieces in MS66 FH and MS67 FH, both services combined, on this "common" date. I have placed several of the MS66 FH's and almost without exception, the full head noted on the holder was accurate. This date is usually snow or blast white in MS65 FH and MS66 FH. This "common" date coin is not so common after you factor in the number of break-outs sent back to the services. Almost without exception the third and fourth rivets are weak and there are rarely any vertical or horizontal shield lines visible.

1929-D

Mintage: 1,358,000

Price Rank—11
Quantity Rank—5

G	VG	F	VF	XF	AU	BU	GEM
20%	15%	15%	15%	15%	10%	5%	5%

2% STRUCK WITH FULL HEADS

The 1929-D is certainly an underrated coin. The Guidebook prices this coin about 25% above the common date, but according to the "price and quantity chart" in this book, you can see the 1929-D is not shown in its true light. Full Head Standing Liberty Quarters of this date are very scarce. This date could be compared closely to the 1928-D. There are many 1929-D quarters, uncirculated, on the market, but probably one percent or less would fit this category of price and quality.

There are 478,000 less made of this date than the 1919-S, yet the 1919-S MS65 Full Head is currently valued at $28,000. 1995 prices for 1929-D are $7500/$7900 in MS 65FH. An MS 66FH recently changed hands for $22,000. Got any??

GRADING:

OBVERSE

A lot of these exist that are "close, but no cigar" 90-95% head. With close scrutiny, the temple and throat of Miss Liberty are not FULLY separated. May lack in only a very small area- but NOT A FULL HEAD. LOOK CAREFULLY! Much weaker than normal strike. Much flatness on Miss Liberty's torso from her waist to her knee. Look for any slide marks if you are buying M.S. 60 to M.S. 63.

REVERSE

Usually weakly struck on the eagle's breast as well as left wing. ANY circulation will make the coin look like an XF or even a VF.

* * *

AVAILABILITY OF FULL HEADS:

		MS65	MS66	MS67
FULL HEADS:	PCGS	16	2	0
	NGC	7	0	0
NON-FULL HEADS:				
	PCGS	84	15	0
	NGC	31	9	1

Have had the pleasure of viewing both of the P.C.G.S. MS66 FH's. Each is white with a sharp full head. One of the pieces was an upgrade from an MS65 FH that was purchased at one of the West coast auctions. The other MS66 FH was submitted for encapsulation by a collector out West and was raw when submitted. I have handled and placed about twelve of the remaining twenty-three pieces at both services. I disagree with the full head designation on nearly one-half of the pieces, so as I tell other collectors: "If you do not agree with the grade on the holder, do not buy the coin".

1929-S

Mintage: 1,764,000

Price Rank—37
Quantity Rank—11

G	VG	F	VF	XF	AU	BU	GEM
15%	15%	15%	15%	10%	15%	10%	5%

5% OR SO STRUCK WITH FULL HEADS

The 1929-S, as most "S" mints, were average or poor strikes. Full Heads are an exception and certainly not a rule. Full Heads are worth two to three times normal catalog when compared to average or flat strikes. This date and mintmark would closely compare to the 1930-S which another author says "is never found" in Full Head. But not so.

Early in 1975, there was a hoard of five rolls of the 1929-S quarters surfaced in California and they were very quickly absorbed into the market without affecting the Full Head demand to any degree. Of the five rolls, there were less than fifty pieces with Full Heads. These seem to be put away in 1929. Your author personally examined many of those pieces and was delighted to see an "S" mint on the market with a true Full Head.

GRADING:

OBVERSE

Usually stronger strike than most "S" mints, but lacking in head detail. Look for any circulation signs; i.e. amber areas on shield or Miss Liberty's bust, or her knee.

REVERSE

Better than average "S" mint, though not strongly struck. You can expect much detail in the eagle's feathers except the edge of the eagle's left wing.

* * *

AVAILABILITY OF FULL HEADS:

		MS65	MS66	MS67
FULL HEADS:	PCGS	106	19	0
	NGC	60	16	1
NON-FULL HEADS:				
	PCGS	180	41	1
	NGC	107	37	2

With 36 pieces in MS66 FH and MS67 FH, there seems to be enough to supply today's collectors' demands. We placed the lone MS67 FH piece into the hands of a very astute collector. It was a beautifully toned medium to light golden, with russet and rose, with an outstanding full head. It seems that many of the MS65 FH and MS66 FH pieces were the early grading, and in my opinion would not grade full head under today's stricter guidelines and requirements.

As is frequently the case with "S" mints, the 1929-S lacks a bit in either the temple or ear area. At times, the ear hole is very faint or missing. I have placed approximately seventy-five pieces of these from both services, and at the risk of repeating myself too often: "if I do not agree with the grade, I do not handle it".

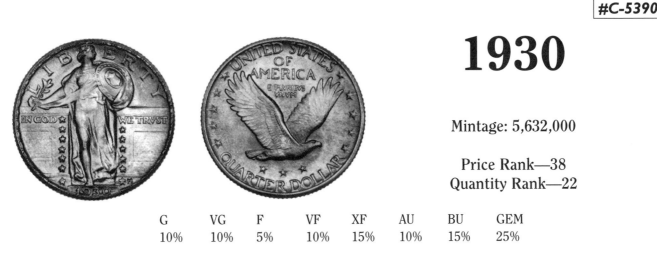

1930

Mintage: 5,632,000

Price Rank—38
Quantity Rank—22

G	VG	F	VF	XF	AU	BU	GEM
10%	10%	5%	10%	15%	10%	15%	25%

50% STRUCK WITH FULL HEADS

The 1930 is probably the most available of all Standing Liberty Quarters in Full Head except 1917-Ty. I. If any date and mintmark could be called "common", this is it, with probably 50% struck with Full Heads. Much in demand (especially for Type collectors) for the Type III Full Head Standing Liberty Quarter. Type III is the recessed date that begins in 1925 and carries through 1930. Type collectors usually go for the first or last coin issued.

GRADING:

OBVERSE

THE strongest strike of all Standing Liberty Quarters, with the highest number of Full Heads available. Head will be full, frequently, on many AU's-some even on XF. Almost the model for grading; but you can't expect the other years to look this strong. Shield is usually full as well. All rivets should be there.

REVERSE

Usually strong (as many "Philly" mints are). Even breast feathers are better struck than most other years. Frequently comes frosty or milky white and/or with a beautiful cartwheel effect.

* * *

AVAILABILITY OF FULL HEADS:

		MS65	MS66	MS67
FULL HEADS:	PCGS	325	69	10
	NGC	139	14	0
NON-FULL HEADS:				
	PCGS	104	24	0
	NGC	38	6	0

A statement made in my first "Standing Liberty Quarters" book published in 1975 still holds true. The 1930 is "probably the most available of all Standing Liberty Quarters in Full Head except the 1917 Type "I". In MS65 FH, MS66 FH and MS67 FH the total number of pieces encapsulated by both services is a whopping 557 pieces at this writing. Only 172 pieces in MS65, and MS66, and MS67 non-full heads. Wow! What a contrast.

I have placed approximately one-half of the MS67 FH's and lost count of the MS65 FH and MS66 FH numbers. Most were very white and some were just a bit shy of a true sharp full head. Overall, it seems that in the early days the grading services were a bit more lenient in grading the full head status on pieces; particularly in the ear area. I have tried to cross several pieces from one service to the other but with no luck?

1930-S

Mintage: 1,556,000

Price Rank—30
Quantity Rank—8

G	VG	F	VF	XF	AU	BU	GEM
12%	10%	15%	20%	15%	15%	10%	3%

1% OR LESS STRUCK WITH FULL HEADS

Since the mint anticipated this would be the last year for the Standing Liberty Quarter, new dies were not shipped to the branch mints from the mother mint, Philadelphia, Pennsylvania, as quickly as they would have been ordinarily. Worn dies were used much beyond their ordinary usage, which accounts, in part for so many flat heads. It is frequently compared side-by-side with the 1930-P. SHOULD NOT BE!! True worth should be three to five times scarcer. The mintage alone bears this out. 1,556,000 vs 5,632,000. Full Heads come about one fifth as often as the 1930-P. Much, much underrated in M.S. 65/ 67 Full Head.

It is in print by another well known author that GEM Full Heads are "non-existent" but NOT SO! Many screamers or "monster" coins DO exist. At least two reside in the state of Florida. They are full frosty white. Similar to the frosty proofs of today. I have not seen any others this beautiful in many years. They usually go by private sale, when they do surface, rather than by public auction or sale.

Full Heads of this date are worth many times Guidebook prices, when they do indeed become available. An example would be the 1945-P Mercury Dime with the Split Bands. Coin Dealer Newsletter lists it at $2,250.00 and the Guidebook prices the same coin at $20.00.

GRADING:

OBVERSE

Many soft strikes. Especially in the head and inner shield. Also soft 3rd and 4th rivets on shield. Due consideration should be given in grading this date and mintmark.

REVERSE

Usually very well struck, but NOT SHARP in breast area.

* * *

AVAILABILITY OF FULL HEADS:

		MS65	MS66	MS67
FULL HEADS:	PCGS	92	25	1
	NGC	62	12	2
NON-FULL HEADS:				
	PCGS	137	44	4
	NGC	60	19	2

This is the surprise of the series. Since the slabbing services began their operation in 1986, this has been thought to be very tough and still is much tougher than its sister date, the 1930-P, and should not be paralleled pricewise, either. A total of 194 full head pieces in MS 65 and higher have been encapsulated. This is one of the split at ear varieties and not the regular hole at ear and I think this is the reason there are so many in full head holders. There are precious few pieces that would qualify for the ultimate full head, as they would need the entire tuft under the ear hole, not just the visible split. The tuft should be raised on the ultimate full head pieces, and are quite rare. In several discussions with the grading services, I have been told that full head is just that. Stop with the ear on many of the 1925 to 1930 pieces, and especially the "S" mints.

If you are searching for the ultimate full head on this one, I think you will be looking for a very long time. I have seen fewer than a dozen pieces in all my years of dealing in Standing Liberty Quarters, and most were many years ago. Another author has it in print that there are "none in existence in full head". Wow! Would he get a surprise today.

1931 (???)

Artist's conception of a
1931-P quarter

Having spoken to many respected, knowledgeable and renowned coin dealers throughout the entire country, only a very few have ever heard of the possible existence of this date. Having discussed this matter with the late Jim Kelly and the late Julian Marks, they believed there were some, but tended to be a bit ambiguous at times, since there were no mint records or other recorded proof of the existence of this dated Quarter. It is possible that the late Colonel Green's collection and possibly King Farouk's collection had a 1931-P Standing Liberty Quarter in it. To date, there is no recorded proof of any of these. There is the definite possibility that some do exist. The very large mintage of the 1930 Philadelphia Mint and the 1930 San Francisco Mint convinces some that the mint was expecting to strike a 1931 Standing Liberty Quarter on a production basis. A 1931 master die had already been made, and working dies were waiting for the year to end and the new year to begin.

Since legislation was not passed until March 3, 1931 for the striking of the Washington Quarter, I firmly believe some 1931 coins were struck very similar to the situation in 1964 when 20 million Peace Dollars (during the Johnson administration) were authorized by the U.S. Government to satisfy the gambling casinos of Nevada, only to be melted a few weeks later. All of which did not make it back to the melting pot, as I was offered one several years ago to the tune of $ 15,000. With approximately 8 weeks into the new year, I feel there are some 1931 Standing Liberty Quarters out there and would be delighted to know where???

Chapter 6

"Die Varieties..."
•
"Investment Potential of Extremely Fine Standing Liberty Quarters"

Die Varieties of Standing Liberty Quarters

By Darrel Neidigh

Explanation of S# (10 positions):
  1st. 4: Breen Encyclopedia #
  5th: Code for Major Differences (eg B = A rev. C=B rev.
  6th: Code for Major Variety (eg D/D or doubled die)
  7-10th: Code for a Minor Variety (e.g. clashed die)

Description of Codes for Major Differences (5th position):
  No letter: No Major or Minor Differences or Varieties
  A: No Major Differences, but a Major or Minor Variety
  B thru Y: Sequencing Letters for Major Differences
  Z: Exact Major Difference is Not Known

Description of Codes for Major Varieties (6th position):
  No letter: No Major or Minor Varieties
  A: No Major Variety, but with 1 or More Minor Varieties
  B thru E: RePunched Mintmarks (RPM) Wexler Numbered
  F thru H: RePunched Mintmarks (RPM) Not Wexler Numbered
  I & J: Over Mint Marks (OMM)
  K thru M: Obverse Doubled Dies (sequencing)
  N thru Q: Reverse Doubled Dies (sequencing)
  R thru Y: Others (eg doubled dates) Not listed above
  Z: Exact Major Variety is Not Known

Description of Codes for Minor Varieties (7-10th positions):
  a: Clashed Die, Obverse
  b: Clashed Die, Reverse
  c, d & e: Die Break, Obverse
  f, g & h: Die Break, Reverse
  i: Cud
  j: Rim Defect
  k: Repaired Die
  l: Laminated Planchet
  m: Die Gouge
  n: Polished Die

Description of Reverses
  A Rev: No Stars Under Eagle 1916 P, 1917 PDS
  B Rev: 3 Stars Under Eagle 1917 - 1930 PDS

Description of Obverses
  I   Obv: Undraped, Flush Date. Sprig Close to L, Half Reed above Head, Gown Touches Foot & Not Very
       Rounded - 1916
  II   Obv: Sprig from L, Full Reed Above Head, More Rounded Gown Not Touch Foot, Fingers Separated - 1917
       PDS
  III Obv: Mail Drapery, Flush Date 1917 - 1920 PDS, 1921 P
  IV   Obv: Sharper Head, Clapboards, Leaves, Gown & Shield Lines 1921 - 1923 PS, 1924-D
  V   Obv: Date Thinner & Tapered 50% - 1924 PS
  VI   Obv: Recessed Date 1925 - 1930 PDS

Design Type Marriages

Pair 1: A Rev., I Obv. 1916
Pair 2: A Rev., II Obv. 1917 PDS
Pair 3: B Rev., III Obv. 1917-1920 PDS, 1921 P
Pair 4: B Rev., IV Obv. 1921 - 1923 PS, 1924-D
Pair 5: B Rev., V Obv. 1924 PS
Pair 6: B Rev., VI Obv. 1925 - 1930 PDS

DDM	S#	V
1916	4425B	Matte Proof, 3 Leafs Above L, w/o Initial (unique ?)
	4426C	A Rev., I Obv.
1917	4427BA	A Rev., II Obv.
	4227BR	4427 BA Matte Proof, Hi Relief, Sq.Borders, Wire Edge(6?)
	4230CA	B Rev., III Obv.
	4230ZN	42??? A w/CI ? D. Die Rev. #? (?)
1917-D	4229BA	A Rev., II Obv.
	4232CA	B Rev., III Obv.
	4232CAa	4232AA w/Obverse Clashed Die
	4232CAc	4232CA w/Obv. Crks Rim-Initial-2nd Bot R *(hvy), Bot R (c)
	4232CAc" "	*-2nd Bot R *, Rim-Bot L *, Rim-9, Top R * Down L. "U" (c)
	4232CAc" '	Shaped Drapery-2 top L *-Knee-W, W-Bot Shield Pt. Top (c)
	4232Cac' "	L Shield Pt-Neckline, Top R * Down SW, Rim-under ST——
1917-S	4228BA	A Rev., II Obv.
	4228BAb	4228BA w/Rev CD (shows @ top, heavy under 1st S (States)
	4231BAa	4231BA w/Obverse Clashed Die (E of EPU @ knee)
	4231CA	B Rev., III Obv.
	4232CAa	4321CA w/Obverse Clashed Die (E of EPU @ knee)
1918	4233AA	B Rev., III Obv.
	4233AR	4233AA w/1918/7 (exists ?)
1918-D	4236AA	B Rev., III Obv.
	4236AAc	4236AA w/Obverse Die Crack thru Date SE-NW
	4236AAc"	4236AA w/Obverse Die Crack thru Date SW-NE
	4236AAc'	4236AA w/Obverse Die Crack thru Date East-West
	4236AAd	4236AA w/Obverse Die Crack thru Feet-Rim
	4236AR	4236AA w/1918/7 (exists ?)
1918-S	4234AA	B Rev., III Obv.
	4234AAa	4234AA w/Obverse Clashed Die (E of EPU @ knee)
	4234AAc	4234AA w/Obverse Die Crack to Right of 8
	4235AK"	42345AK w/CI 3 D, Die Obv. #1(8/7)
	4235AK"a	4235AK" w/Obv. Clash Mark Below TR (TRUST)
	4235AK"a"	4235AK"a w/Obv. Double Clash Marks Below TR (TRUST)
	4235AK"a'	4235AK"a" w/Obv. Clash Mark E (EPU) @ Right Knee
	4235AK"a'c	4235AK"a' w/Obv. Crks - RUST, Rim-* (@M)

DDM	S#	V
1919	4237	B Rev., III Obv.
1919-D	4239AA	B Rev., III Obv.
	4239AAc	4239AA w/Obverse Die Crack @ Date
	4239AAcf	4239AAc w/Rev Crks Rim-*-R Wing, Rim-L Wing
	4239AAj	4239AA w/Rim Defect (chipped collar)
	4239AR	4239AA w/Incused Area (round) on Shield (die defect)
1919-S	4238	B Rev., III Obv.
	4238AAa	4238AA w/Clash Mark E (EPU) @ Knee
1920	4240AA	B Rev., III Obv.
	4240AAa	4240AA w/Obv. CD Above Arm Below I
	4240AAg	4240AA w/Rev Crk up L Star-Wing
	4240AAm	4240AA w/Rev Die Gouge (above wing-front of & below beak)
1920-D	4242AA	B Rev., III Obv.
	4242AAc	4242AA w/Obverse Die Crack East-West thru Top of Date
	4242Ac"	4242AA w/Obverse Die Crack Rim-LIBERTY
	4242AAc'	4242AA w/Obverse Die Crack East-West thru Middle of Date
1920-S	4241AA	B Rev., III Obv.
	4241AAa	4241AA w/Clashed Die E (at Knee)
	4241AAi	4241AA w/Obverse Cud (tear drop @ left thigh)
1921	4243BA	B Rev., III Obv.
	4243BAa	4243BA w/Clash Mark E (EPU) @ Knee
	4243BAc	4243BA w/Obverse Crack thru Top of Date
	4243CA	B Rev., IV Obv.
	4243ZAa	4243?A w/Obverse Clashed Die
1923	4244AA	B Rev., IV Obv. (2 is needle sharp & thin - see 1923-S)
	4244AAa	4244AA w/Obverse Clashed Die
1923-S	4245	B Rev., IV Obv. (2 is fat @ base & 1/2 way down curve)
1924	4246	B Rev., V Obv.
1924-D	4248AA	B Rev., IV Obv.
	4248AAc	4248AA w/Obverse Die Crack @ Date
	4248AAm	4248AA w/Gouge M to Eagle's R Wing
1924	S	4247AA B Rev., V Obv.
	4247AAa	4247AA w/Obverse Clashed Die
	4247AAn	4247AA w/Thin Right Leg (polished die ?)
	4247AF	4247AA w/S/S/S (looks like three 3) (COUNTERFEIT)
1925	4249	B Rev., VI Obv.

DDM	S#	V
1926	4250AA	B Rev., VI Obv.
	4250AAa	4250AA w/Obverse Clashed Die
	4250AAc	4250AA w/Obverse Die Crack Gown Fold @ Left Leg
	4250AAk	4250AA w/6 Looks like 8 (repaired die)
1926-D	4252	B Rev., VI Obv.
1926-S	4251AA	B Rev., VI Obv.
	4251AAa	4251AA w/Obverse Clashed Die
	4251AAc	4251AA w/Obverse Crack Rim-Base-R Foot-Base
	4251AAd	4251AA w/Obverse Crack Rim-E-Nose
	4251AAi	4251AA w/Obverse Cud (tear drop @ left thigh)
	4251AR	4251AA w/1926/5 (exists ?)
1927	4253	B Rev., VI Obv.
1927-D	4255	B Rev., VI Obv.
1927-S	4254	B Rev., VI Obv. (S must open & loops equal)
1928	4256AA	B Rev., VI Obv.
	4256AAa	4256AA w/Obverse Clashed Die
1928-D	4260AA	B Rev., VI Obv.
	4260AAa	4260AA w/Obverse Clashed Die
	4260AAd	4260AA w/Obverse Crk thru Head
	4260AB	4260AA w/D/D N #1 (scarce)
	4260AB"	4260AA w/D/D S #2 (elusive)
	4261AI	4260AA w/D/S
	4261AIc	4261AI w/Obverse Crks L *-Pedestal-M, Drapery-Ankle-Rim
1928-S	4257BA	B Rev., VI Obv. Sm S (more R. Lower, not touch star rarer)
	4257BAa	4257BA w/Clash Mark E (EPU) @ knee
	4258CA	B Rev., VI Obv. Large S (touches star on left)
	4258ZAa	425??A w/Obverse Clashed Die
	4258ZF	425??A w/S/S W
	4259CB	4258CA w/S/S # 1 (may be Cline's large/small (scarce)
1929	4262AA	B Rev., VI Obv.
	4262AAa	4262AA w/Obverse Clashed Die "E"
1929-D	4264AA	B Rev., VI Obv.
	4264AR	4264AA w/Doubled Eagle's Right Wing Tip
1929-S	4263	B Rev., VI Obv.
1930	4265AA	B Rev., VI Obv.
	4265AAa	4265AA w/Obverse Clashed Die
	4265AAc	4265AA w/Obverse Crack @ Date
1930-S	4266	B Rev., VI Obv.

HELP: In case you read no further, I would like help in identifying a 1917-S Type I which might be a clashed die. Under the 1st S of STATES is a raised oval of metal slightly smaller than O of OF with a triangular center. It's depth is equal to that of the letter S. Extra metal is to the right of the bottom left star, thru the base of the 4th star up on the left, around the letters UNITED STAT, and O of OE Large cuds are at the left foot of N, I base and D to the south east. Any information would be appreciated.

I have been using a computer to assemble a listing of the varieties of United States coins. It is extremely useful to track inventory, costs and generate "want lists". The basic number is from Breen's *Complete Encyclopedia of U.S. & Colonial Coins*. Each sub-variety is given an individual number by a series of letters as explained in the first part of the listing. Also in the first part are descriptions of Reverses, Obverses and Die (actually hub) Marriages.

Incidently, collection by Die Marriages is another type of collecting that can be interesting and less costly than a date and mint set, especially for obsolete coins.

But back to Standing Liberty Quarters; as can be seen by the list, there are not many deviations in the series. The 2 Reverses combine with 5 Obverses to give 5 Die Marriages. Obverses III, IV & V are minor modifications of Obverse II.

The 1918-S has the only 2 doubled dies and, of course, the 1918/7 is the best known.

RePunched Mintmarks (RPM), as listed by Wexler & Miller in their RPM book, are limited to 1928-D & S. From other sources I have noted a 1924-S S/S/S, a 1928-D D/S and a 1928-S S/S West.

The 1928-S has 2 Series of mint marks, the small (rarer) does not touch the star and a large which touches.

A few cracked and clashed die pieces complete the listing. The clashed die marks are one of the means to authenticate a 1918/7-S.

I would appreciate any additions or corrections to the listing so that I can update it. I will publish any changes with credit to the owner.

Darrel O. Neidigh
405 Topsfield Rd.
Hockessin, DE 19707

The Investment Potential of
Extremely Fine Standing Liberty Quarters

By John Garhammer

Note: This article was originally published in two parts.

Numismatic publications and dealers' advertisements often contain information about the investment potential of coins. The uncirculated coin market gets most of the attention and seems to have the greatest fluctuations, to say nothing about changes in grading standards. My interest lies in top quality XF-AU Standing Liberty Quarters. To evaluate what investment potential these coins may have, I've looked back over thirty years of *Red Book* values for XF Standing Liberty Quarters. Note that this type of analysis is all but impossible with uncirculated coins since grading scales of MS60-70 are a fairly recent development. What I found was interesting to me and may be to you as well; thus, I've put this article together to share the insights. The data presented below were assembled for my own interest and are offered for your inspection. The opinions given are mine alone, and I am but a part time collector. Any comments would be welcomed to the letter section of Mac Neil's Notes. First, a brief description of how I became interested in Standing Liberty Quarters.

My father was a bus driver back in the days when bus drivers handled real money, coins that is. I don't remember how I started, but by the age of about 12 1 looked through my dad's coins every day when he came home from work. This was the early 1960's, when you could find a few Standing Liberty Quarters in circulation (1925-30-P with an occasional mint mark). I saved all varieties of coins from quarters to pennies, but could not afford halves, let alone silver dollars. Washington quarters were my main focus since it was possible to assemble a complete collection from circulation, although over the years my dad and I found only a few 32-D or S quarters. I was, however, most interested in Standing Liberty Quarters, but realized that there was no hope of finding more that about a third of the series in circulation. Since I barely had the money to save what I wanted from circulation "finds," I couldn't buy many coins.

Nevertheless, mostly via my home town coin club and a local dealer, I did buy, sell and trade some coins. I decided to try to assemble as complete a Standing Liberty Quarter collection as I could. I had found about ten different dates/mints (G-F grade) from circulation, and bought almost as many, mostly for two to three dollars. Thus, I had assembled about half a complete set. My prized Standing Liberty Quarter was a 1926P AU FH, which I bought (as UNC) on June 26, 1964. I had no idea what a full head was back then, but asked my local dealer to sell me "one real nice Standing Liberty Quarter, with all the detail." It cost me five dollars, and is the only coin from my original Standing Liberty Quarter book that resides in my current collection #1! Then came college, etc., etc. For over twenty years my coins sat and waited. In October 1986 I saw an ad for the Long Beach Coin & Stamp Expo. Not living very far away I decided to attend and happened to walk by J. Cline's table. That was it, I spent over $100 at that show on Standing Liberty Quarters (which was a lot for someone who last paid $5 for an almost UNC Standing Lib.). Since then I've been

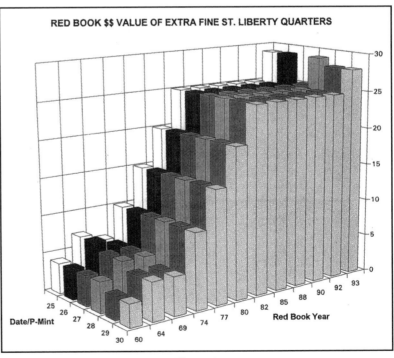

Figure I

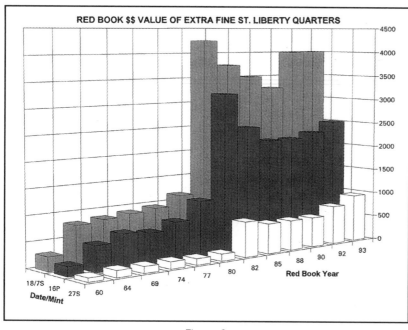

RED BOOK $$ VALUE OF EXTRA FINE ST. LIBERTY QUARTERS

Figure 2

Both the 1916 and 1918/7-S quarters made steady value increases from 1960 to 1980, with a four to five fold gain. As with the 27-S, these coins made large advances during the 1980 market surge, increasing in value by a factor of three to four in two years. As is obvious, those who invested in the late seventies were happy people in the early eighties! Prices receded during the eighties, but advanced upward toward their record highs by the early nineties. Overall, these two key coins increased in value nearly 15 fold from 1960 to 1993. What's that rule? Invest in truly rare coins in the highest grade you can afford!

In Part 2 of this article, in the next issue of Mac Neil's Notes, I will discuss the semi-key Standing Liberty Quarters (19-D&S, 21, 23-S) and a few that seem to have had an unusual value record over the years. A performance comparison with the key Washington Quarter (1932-D) will also be made.

PART 2

In Part 1 of this article I discussed the value growth of the key date Standing Liberty Quarters, as well as that of the most common date coins in the series. All values were based on the annual *Red Book* list price for extra fine grade coins. Reasons for analyzing this grade over the years were given in Part 1. It was shown that value increases from 1960 to 1993 indicated that the coins evaluated represented good investments, particularly during the period from just before 1980 to just after the coin market surge of that year It should be emphasized that the *Red Book* values represent typical coins, as opposed to "blazers" that have full heads or other exceptional device details. The recent article in Mac Neil's Notes by Joe Abbin (Volume III, # 2, pages 3-7) indicated that full head Standing Liberty Quarters may command one and a half to many times the price of non full head examples of specific dates in uncirculated grades. Some of this value inflation filters down to the XF grades. I recently bought a 1924-D AU quarter at the Long Beach Expo for less than $100. The dealer had a few AU 1924-D full head specimens for sale in the $400-$500 range! Thus, if an investor had purchased some of this type of higher quality coin years ago, the value increases would likely be many times that indicated by Figures 1 and 2 in Part 1 and the Figures discussed below.

I would like to supplement the discussion that

trying to upgrade my #1 set to a strong XF-AU collection.

Figure 1 shows the *Red Book* value progression from 1960-1993 for the most common (1925-30-P) XF Standing Liberty Quarters. A fairly steady price increase is evident from 1960 until the early 80's. This is followed by a flat decade with a small increase evident in the 1993 values. Since the *Red Book* value data is assembled more than a year before the cover date, the 1993 increase is likely a reflection of the 1989-90 surge in the coin market, and not representative of the current market (Fall 1992). The data of Figure 1 indicates that an investment made in these inexpensive common date Standing Liberty Quarters in the early 1960's would have increased about six fold by today's values. Not a great growth record, but comparable to a savings account yielding 8% interest compounded quarterly, which would require almost 23 years to result in the same six fold increase. In addition to the value increase, however, one should consider the pleasures involved with coin collecting and the lack of yearly income taxes!

Figure 2 shows the *Red Book* value progression from 1960-1993 for the key Standing Liberty Quarters. The 1927-S values were stable for about 20 years, prior to the 1980 coin market surge. That surge resulted in a five fold increase in value in a two year period. In the last decade the 27-S values receded slightly and then recovered ground to register a new high in the most recent *Red Book* issue. The almost twelve fold value increase since 1960, and six to seven fold increase since 1980, would be acceptable to most investors.

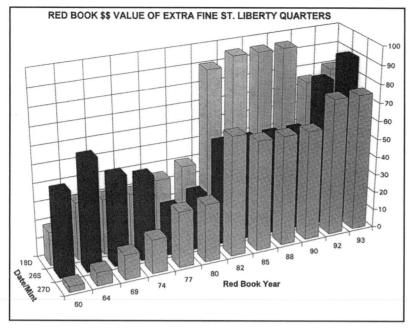

RED BOOK $$ VALUE OF EXTRA FINE ST. LIBERTY QUARTERS

Figure 3

time in the late seventies.

The 1918-D has a mintage of about two and a half times that of the 1926-S (7.38 to 2.70 million), but was minted during the non-recessed date era of the series. Starting at $18 in 1960, its value climbed to $40 in 1980, but then more than doubled to $90 in 1982. It remained close to that level for nearly a decade before dropping to $75 in 1992 and then rising slightly to $80 in 1993. Overall, a near four fold increase from 1960 and a small decrease since 1982 did not make this coin a good investment choice.

Figure 4 shows the *Red Book* value progression from 1960-1993 for the semi-key Standing Liberty Quarters (19-D & S, 21-P and 23-S). All four of these coins made modest value gains from 1960 to 1980 and then roughly doubled from 1980 to 1982. Since then the 21-P and 19-D have been relatively stable in value, while the 19-S has surged upward in 1992 and 93. The 23-S gained over $100 from 1982 to 1985 and held its peak value until 1992 and 93 when moderate decreases occurred. Overall during the 33 year period the 23-S increased nearly six fold, the 21-P and 19-S about five fold, and the 19-D ten fold due to its low 1960 value.

Figures 1, 2, 3 & 4 and the discussion in this two

accompanied Figure 1 in Part 1 of this article by pointing out that the 1928 and 1929-D and S mint, and the 1930-S coins have very similar value growth records to those shown for the 1925-30 P mint coins. Their values are from zero to seven dollars higher than the corresponding P mint coins in the 1993 *Red Book*.

Figure 3 shows the *Red Book* value progression from 1960-1993 for the 1927-D, 1926-S and 1918-D quarters. The 1927-D, despite its low mintage of slightly less than one million (which has been questioned by J.H. Cline on page 157 of the revised edition of his book) and a ten fold value increase from 1960, listed at only $31 in 1980. By 1982 its value more than doubled to $65 (the 1927-S increased by a factor of five over the same two year period, see Figure 2). It's value was then rather steady for about ten years but has increased to $75 for 1992 and 1993. This is a net 25 fold increase since 1960!

The 1926-S has one of the more interesting value histories. It was one of the more highly valued coins in the series during the sixties but then dropped to about half its former value by 1980. It regained and held its sixty's value during the eighties, but then almost doubled this value by 1993. Early investment in this coin provided a rollercoaster ride, with only a three fold increase if purchased at the optimum

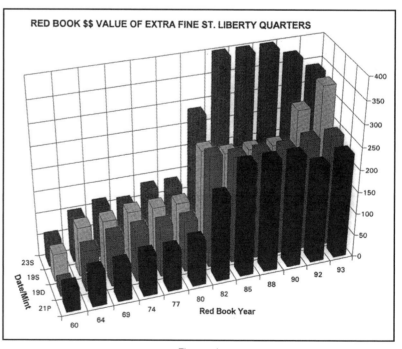

RED BOOK $$ VALUE OF EXTRA FINE ST. LIBERTY QUARTERS

Figure 4

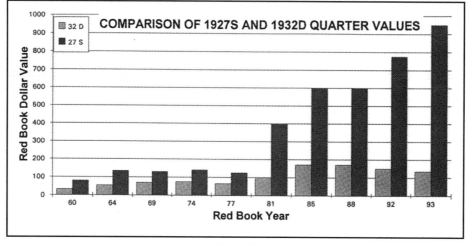

Figure 5

part article have shown that investment in XF grade Standing Liberty Quarters in 1960 would have been a good one. The 1927-D produced the greatest gains (25 fold increase), with the key date coins (16 P, 18/7-S and 27-S) growing in value by a factor of 12 to 15. Surprisingly, the semi-key dates of Figure 4 performed in a manner comparable to the (forgotten) common dates of Figure 1. Thus, there is a price range for every investor. Timing was certainly an important consideration, such as 1980 vs. 1982 prices, but low mintage in a

quality grade long term investment proved to be the real winning combination.

Figure 5 compares the value growth of the 1927-S Standing Liberty and 1932-D Washington Quarters, which have a similar mintage quantity and date. There is clearly no investment comparison. Why? There may be several reasons but I offer only one. Look at the artistic content on the obverse and at the eagle position and detail on the reverse of each coin. See what I mean?

Chapter 7

GRADING

As in the past, I still emphasize eye appeal considerably. This is one of the reasons you are drawn to a certain coin over another. It "draws" your eye with luster, color, strike, etc. Remember, if you do not like it do not buy it!

There are several things to keep in mind when grading the 1916 quarter. The hair design on the 1916 is different than the succeeding 1917 Ty.I. On the 1916, the last three curls fall forward in Miss Liberty's hair and many of the pieces are lacking in detail in the hair or are softly struck (whichever term you prefer.) The shield lines on the 1916 are very weak, both vertical and horizontal, as are the rivets on the top half of the shield. When grading Full Heads, there is one curl above Miss Liberty's ear which must come to a horizontal "V" to be classified Full Head.

M.S. 67

OBVERSE

Virtually perfect in every respect. Outstanding strike with gorgeous eye appeal. Brilliant or satiny although many 1916's are a beautiful russet color. Full hair separation from forehead to back of Liberty's head. Shield can be full although never sharp and rivets are weak. Toes will be separated. SPECIAL NOTE: The reason for the softness in strikes on the 1916's is that all dies set from July, 1916 until December, 1916 before any coins were struck. Those dies became rusty and so just before the first strikes were made in December the dies had to be cleaned with an abrasive such as emery cloth or crocus cloth to remove the rust. This abrasive cleaning "deadened" the features slightly on the dies. The rivets on the 1916 are nearly always weak and/or flattened particularly along Miss Liberty's body.

REVERSE

Frequently on the 1916, the reverse will be 1/2 to a full grade better than the obverse. Eagle will be fully struck in every respect. Breast, wing edges, tail feathers and talons. All will be clear and distinct.

M.S. 65

OBVERSE

No distracting bag marks, and certainly not in critical areas. Very minute marks, only. Eye appeal should be excellent. Overall strike is weaker (see special note above). Almost never satiny. Light, medium or heavy russet toning is normal on the 1916. A fainter line of separation for the full head is the norm, with a hole in hair at the ear.

REVERSE:

Fully struck on eagle's breast feathers and wings. Pinfeathers or edges of wings may be weakly struck.

M.S. 64

OBVERSE

Miniscule bagmarks and blemishes begin to appear in this grade. Still should not be in critical places such as face, neck, leg or shield. Nicer eye appeal than an MS 63 and toning should be even on obverse and reverse.

REVERSE:

Eagle's breast feathers weak but full, and pin feathers on the very edges of the wings may be weak. Somewhat flat on chest of eagle. Fold of skin over eagle's eye usually complete.

M.S. 63

OBVERSE

A few more bagmarks or blemishes than the MS 64 grade, but still should have nice eye appeal. Decent strike in the breast, shield, knee and head. Strike is average for a 1916 in this uncirculated grade.

REVERSE:

Eagle's breast, tail feathers and wings are a touch more softly struck than on the MS 64.

M.S. 60

OBVERSE

A true, uncirculated coin. New with no evidence of wear, but does have some bagmarks. Usually softly struck in the knee, shield, left bust and head. Flatness on the knee may appear to the untrained eye as wear. The flatness must not have the tiny lines caused by circulation. This can be a close call. MS 60 may be mottled or heavily toned. Head will almost always be flat in this grade.

REVERSE

Weakly struck eagle's breast, tail feathers and wings (particularly the left wing). Do not confuse with wear. Again, flatness of strike cannot have the tiny lines caused by circulation to be uncirculated.

Author's note: On any circulated grade, AG-AU any unnatural discoloration, rim ding, cleaning, buffing scrapes or scratches is expected to lower the grade by as little as one grade or as much as three or four grades. Depends on the severity of the problem as well as the location.

AU—ABOUT UNCIRCULATED, 55

OBVERSE

Just a trace of rub or wear on the very highest points; i.e. knee, shield, left breast and head.

REVERSE

Just a touch of wear on eagle's breast and right wing feathers. 80-90% mint luster remains. Also wear spots may have a hint of amber or brown (off color) as compared to the rest of the coin. Many pieces in this grade are bought and sold as uncirculated. CAUTION!!!

AU— About Uncirculated, 50

OBVERSE

Progressed wear on all the above points, especially the knee. Less luster and eye appeal than AU55.

REVERSE

Just a touch of wear on center of breast and edge of wing.

XF—EXTRA FINE, 45

OBVERSE

Where light traces of rub were, now there are flat spots— gown, knee, head, shield, toes, left bust. Gown lines will be weak, but defined. Bust will be about 1/2 flat.

REVERSE

Eagle's breast shows flat spots as well. Eagle's right wing (front edge) will have flat spots as well.

XF—EXTRA FINE, 40

OBVERSE

Breast, right leg, head, shield show much wear. About 1/2 of Miss Liberty's gown lines will be worn away.

REVERSE

Eagle's breast about 1/2 worn away as well as eagle's right wing will be flat from body to first long flight feather. Should still have 20-30% mint luster.

VF—VERY FINE, 30

OBVERSE

Considerable wear spots on breast, shield, leg and head. Worn flat from top of foot to half way up thigh where gown crosses thigh. Only a few gown lines show. Inner circle on shield will be weak.

REVERSE

Eagle's right wing or breast are worn, but most major details remain, especially feathers in middle portions of wings — "V" between eagle's two wings must be complete. Should expect some mint luster—but only around the devices.

VF—VERY FINE, 20

OBVERSE

Miss Liberty's right leg worn flat from top of foot to thigh, but a small amount of gown lines show in waist to bust area. Most rivets on outer shield show, though some will be weak near Miss Liberty's body.

REVERSE

Most major details show, but eagle is quite worn. Both wings are worn nearly flat, but about 1/3 or less of the feathers show.

F—FINE, 15

OBVERSE

For all intents and purposes gown is worn smooth, except in deepest folds along Liberty's body. Right leg is flat usually toes as well. Especially on her right foot. Date is usually clear, but top 1/3 is worn away. Full rim. Drapery on Miss Liberty's torso faint, but there.

REVERSE

Eagle outlined with about 1/3 of feathers showing in the deepest recesses of the wings but little or no details.

VG—VERY GOOD, 8

OBVERSE

Only the major detail shows. Little or no detail in gown except edges from waist to feet. Liberty will be worn into rim, and maybe some of the letters on reverse as well. About 1/2 of drape across Miss Liberty's waist is visible. Date will be 1/2 to 2/3 complete. Should be even wear across the top of date.

REVERSE

1/3 or less of eagle's feathers show, though flight feathers on tips of wings are still separated. Rim should be complete.

G—GOOD, 4

OBVERSE

Heavily worn with little or no detail showing. Legend and date weak but discernible.

REVERSE

Eagle may be worn flat, but completely outlined. Stars and letters will be weak and worn into rim in several spots.

AG—ABOUT GOOD, 3*

OBVERSE

Most details worn smooth. Liberty weak. Most stars weak or missing. Legs worn together. Not all of date will be readable.

REVERSE

Eagle, letters and legend almost worn off completely.

NOTE: This grade is not recommended in Standing Liberty Quarters by this author—not for this date or even the overdate.

M.S. 67

OBVERSE

Virtually perfect in every respect. Outstanding strike with satiny cartwheel effect. Full and rounded head. Rounded cheeks and hair separation from forehead to back of Miss Liberty's head. Shield and toes full and complete.

REVERSE

Eagle must be fully struck: breast, wing edges, tail feathers, talons. All must be clear and distinct.

M.S. 65

OBVERSE

Nearly perfect with no distracting bagmarks and certainly never in obvious places. Very minute if any exist. Excellent eye appeal. Great overall strike. Light golden or satiny finish normal for this grade. Full Head for this type is: a distinct line between hair and forehead as well as temple and neck. Hole in hair at ear. The french bun hair portion may be rounded somewhat, but rarely raised.

REVERSE

Fully struck eagle's breast feathers and wings. Pin feathers or wing edges may be weakly struck.

M.S. 64

OBVERSE

Bagmarks and blemishes are miniscule and should not be in obvious places such as face, neck, leg and shield. Usually much more eye appeal than an MS 63 piece and a stronger strike. Should have nice even toning overall.

REVERSE

Feathers on eagle's breast full, although some on the very edges of the wings may exhibit some weakness. Overall, the reverse should be well struck. Breast feathers complete with no flat chest; not even in the center of the breast. Fold of skin above eagle's eye complete.

M.S. 63

OBVERSE

Nice piece. Uncirculated and with nice eye appeal. A few more bagmarks and blemishes than the MS 64 grade. Good strike in breast, shield, knee and head, although not as strong as MS 64 in these areas.

REVERSE

Nice eye appeal. Some bagmarks and blemishes, but a good strike overall. Most feathers on breast and wings.

M.S. 60

OBVERSE

A true, uncirculated coin. No evidence of wear whatsoever. Usually a softer strike in knee area, head, shield and left bust. Again, as with the 1916, flatness on knee may appear to be wear. An uncirculated coin cannot have the tiny lines on that flatness. Can be mottled or heavily toned in this grade. This is the classic strong strike of the series. About 70-80% struck with Full Heads.

REVERSE

Eagle's breast, tail feathers and wings will be more weakly struck. Do not confuse with wear! Again, look for the tiny lines on the flat area. Uncirculated pieces cannot have the tiny lines. When circulated, the high spots usually have an amber/light brown cast and appear off-color.

AU—ABOUT UNCIRCULATED, 55

OBVERSE

Just a trace of rub or wear on the very highest points; i.e. knee, shield, left breast and head.

REVERSE

Just a touch of wear on eagle's breast and right wing feathers. 80-90% mint luster remains. Also wear spots may have a hint of amber or brown (off color) as compared to the rest of the coin. Many pieces in this grade are bought and sold as uncirculated. CAUTION!!!

AU—ABOUT UNCIRCULATED, 50

OBVERSE

Progressed wear on all the above points, with less luster and much less eye appeal.

REVERSE

Just a touch of wear on center of breast and edge of wing.

XF—EXTRA FINE, 45

OBVERSE

Where light traces of rub were, now there are flat spots— gown, knee, head, shield, toes, left bust. Gown lines will be weak, but defined. Bust will be about 1/2 flat.

REVERSE

Eagle's breast shows flat spots as well. Eagle's right wing (front edge) will have flat spots as well.

XF—EXTRA FINE, 40

OBVERSE

Breast, right leg, head, shield show much wear. About 1/2 of Miss Liberty's gown lines will be worn away.

REVERSE

Eagle's breast about 1/2 worn away as well as eagle's right wing will usually be flat from body to first long flight feather. Should still have 30-50% of mint luster.

VF—VERY FINE, 30

OBVERSE

Considerable wear spots on breast, shield, leg and head. Worn flat from top of foot to about half way up the thigh where the gown crosses. Only a few gown lines remain visible. Inner circle on shield will be weak but must be complete.

REVERSE

Eagle's right wing or breast are worn, but most major details remain, especially feathers in middle portions of wings — "V" between eagle's two wings must be complete. Should expect some mint luster—but only around the devices.

VF—VERY FINE, 20

OBVERSE

Miss Liberty's right leg worn flat from top of foot to thigh, but a small amount of gown lines show in waist to bust area. Most rivets on outer shield show, though some will be weak near Miss Liberty's body.

REVERSE

Most major details show, but eagle is quite worn. Both wings are worn nearly flat, but about 1/3 or less of the feathers show.

F—FINE, 15

OBVERSE

For all intents and purposes gown is worn smooth, except in deepest folds along Liberty's body. Right leg is flat usually toes as well. Especially on her right foot. Date is usually clear, but top 1/3 is worn away. Full rim. Drapery on Miss Liberty's torso faint, but there.

REVERSE

Eagle outlined with about 1/3 of feathers showing in the deepest recesses of the wings but little or no details.

VG—VERY GOOD, 8

OBVERSE

Only the major detail shows. Little or no detail in gown except edges from waist to feet. Liberty will be worn into rim, and maybe some of the letters on reverse as well. About 1/2 of drape across Miss Liberty's waist is visible. Date will be 1/2 to 2/3 complete. Should be even wear across the top of date.

REVERSE

1/3 or less of eagle's feathers show, though flight feathers on tips of wings are still separated. Rim should be complete.

G—GOOD, 4

OBVERSE

Heavily worn with little or no detail showing. Legend and date weak but discernible.

REVERSE

Eagle may be worn flat, but completely outlined. Stars and letters will be weak and worn into rim in several spots.

AG—ABOUT GOOD, 3*

OBVERSE

Most details worn smooth. Liberty weak. Most stars weak or missing. Legs worn together. Not all of date will be readable.

REVERSE

Eagle, letters and legend almost worn off completely.

*NOTE: This grade is not recommended in Standing Liberty Quarters by this author—not even the 1916 or the overdate.

M.S. 70

OBVERSE & REVERSE

Virtually nonexistent. Perfect in every respect.

M.S. 67

OBVERSE

Virtually perfect in every respect. Outstanding strike. Gorgeous eye appeal. Brilliant. Satiny, light golden or cartwheel effect. Full and rounded head and olive leaves. Rounded cheek and hair separation from forehead to back of head.

REVERSE

Outstanding in every respect. All feathers complete and strong, including the twin breast bone on the eagle will be rounded. See the ultimate elsewhere in this book.

M.S. 65

OBVERSE

No distracting bagmarks whatsoever—very minute if at all. Usually nice eye appeal. Overall strike is much improved. Light golden to satiny look is normal in this grade. Certain dates have a head lacking in detail. Full Head detail includes: a distinct line between Liberty's hair and forehead, as well as temple and neck. The three olive leaves are complete. Hole in hair where ear is. The three olive leaves at Liberty's temple ear fused together at base and almost never raised, except the very first 5-10 pieces struck from new dies.

M.S. 64

OBVERSE

Bagmarks and blemishes are miniscule and certainly not in obvious places, such as face, neck, knee, shield or field. Usually much stronger strike and detail is improved as well as improved eye appeal over M.S. 63 grade.

REVERSE

Eagle's breast feathers are usually complete on this grade. May lack in center or have very few bag marks in the wrong places.

M.S. 63

OBVERSE

A little better strike than M.S. 60, i.e.: head, shield and knee will show a little more definition. Usually some eye appeal begins to show in this grade. Shield and chain mail improve over M.S. 60.

REVERSE

Eagle's breast is improved, especially in detail, but still weak. Maybe evenly toned, but not always on this grade.

M.S. 60

OBVERSE

An absolutely new coin with no trace of wear, but with many bagmarks, uneven toning or undesirable toning. May be dull to mottled toning. Shield, head, knee frequently flatly or weakly struck at best. Frequently 3rd or 4th rivets on outer shield weak or missing.

REVERSE

Eagle's breast feathers usually weak, as well as left wing feathers. Head and beak will be weak, also. Maybe unevenly toned or mottled and/or bag marks.

AU—ABOUT UNCIRCULATED, 55

OBVERSE

Just a trace of wear or rub on the very highest points such as the knee, shield, chain mail design on left breast, and head. Also in drapery in her right hand at the wrist area. Should expect 80-90% mint luster.

REVERSE

Just a touch of wear on eagle's breast and right wing edge from eagle's body to first flight feather.

AU—ABOUT UNCIRCULATED, 50

OBVERSE

Progressed wear on all the above points with much less luster and much less eye appeal.

REVERSE

Worn spots on center breast feathers as well as wings. Tail feathers show some wear on the edges. On more weakly struck dates (such as the '27-S, '26-S, '18/7-S, '19-D, 19-S, and '18-D) the top two tail feathers may be together. This is mostly from strike, not wear.

XF—EXTRA FINE, 45

OBVERSE

Where light traces of wear or rub were, there are now worn spots or flat areas from wear. About all gown lines should show, except the twin fold above Miss Liberty's leg. Chain mail on breast is flat in spots.

REVERSE

Worn spots on eagle's front wing edges and breast feathers. Tail feathers should be nearly complete.

XF—EXTRA FINE, 40

OBVERSE

A goodly amount of wear shows on right leg—about 1/2 to 2/3 Of her leg worn flat. Most gown lines worn away much less than the XF 45/ 45.

REVERSE

Right wing edges worn nearly smooth as well as eagle's breast. Right wing will be worn smooth from body to first flight wing feathers. About half of tail feathers show.

VF—VERY FINE, 30

OBVERSE

Considerable wear on shield, leg and breast. Right leg worn from ankle to thigh, but should still be rounded. Some gown lines show on torso. Inner shield circle complete. Drawn drapery across Miss Liberty's body should be complete—no worn spots.

REVERSE

Flight feather on right wing shows, but little or no details. Breast and right wing have a line of separation.

VF—VERY FINE, 20

OBVERSE

Miss Liberty's right leg nearly flat, hip to toes. Progressed wear from 30/30. Especially head, breast, foot and shield. Rivets on outer design of shield complete (except 3rd and 4th ones on weak strikes). Shield's inner circle complete, though weak.

REVERSE

Only major details show, though eagle is worn nearly flat. Few, if any, feathers show in wings except left center of wing.

F—FINE, 15

OBVERSE

Only major outlines show. Most gown lines worn smooth except those close to Liberty's body. Right leg and toe flat. Some chain mail may show. Some weakness at top of date, but very readable. Little or no design left in shield. Only outer rim shows.

REVERSE

Full rim. Letters clearly separated from rim. Outline of eagle only. Usually no feathers show.

VG - VERY GOOD, 8

OBVERSE

Most details worn smooth. Entire design is weak. Most letters are weak as well as date. About 1/3 is worn off. Some lines of drapery across midsection of Liberty, but not complete. Complete rim.

REVERSE

All letters are clear and separate from rim, though some may be weaker than others. "V" is complete on eagle's wing separation. Eagle is outlined and tips of wings (flight feathers) are legible. Not worn together.

G—GOOD, 4

OBVERSE

Very little detail remains. Entire design virtually gone except for major details. "In God we trust" readable. Date weak and may be missing about 1/2 of digits—but must be discernable. Rim worn into letters in spots. Nearly complete.

REVERSE

Eagle worn flat. Only outlined letters and stars worn flat as well. Rim is not complete. Some letters worn into rim.

AG—ABOUT GOOD, 3*

OBVERSE

Figure outlined only. Letters and rim worn together. All around the perimeter. Date about gone, but enough to make it out. (Maybe??) First and second digits frequently weak or worn away on date.

REVERSE

Rim gone and about 1/2 of letter as well. Eagle discernable. "V" of wings worn away as well. Not recommended in this grade by your author.

NOTE: This grade is not recommended by your author for collecting or investment.

Grading Criteria for 1925-1930 Type III Quarters

M.S. 70

OBVERSE and REVERSE

Perfect in every respect. Virtually a non-existent coin.

M.S. 67

OBVERSE

Virtually perfect in every respect. Outstanding strike. Gorgeous eye appeal. Brilliant. Satiny or light golden and/or cartwheel effect. Full and rounded head and olive leaves. Rounded cheeks and hair separation from forehead to back of head. Shield full and complete. All lines, vertical and horizontal, in shield. All toes complete. This description would almost never be true of: 1916, 1918/7-S, 1919-D, 1920-S, 1926-D, 1926-S, 1927-S. (See the section devoted to the connoisseur written for C.D.N. 2/86.) But there are exceptions to every rule.

REVERSE

Eagle will be full feathered. Pinfeathers and talons included. Sharp in every detail.

M.S. 65

OBVERSE Incl. Full Head Description

No distracting bagmarks whatsoever and certainly not in obvious places. Very minute, if at all. Very nice eye appeal. Overall, strike much improved. Light golden or satiny look is normal for this grade. But on 1926-S, 1926-D, 1927-S, 1928-S and 1929-D—almost certain to lack in head detail and not unusual to lack in shield, knee or mail details as well. Full Head detail includes: A distinct line between hair and forehead as well as temple and neck (many so-called "full heads" lack in this area). Hole in hair where ear is. The three olive leaves fused together at base and almost never rounded except the first 10-25 pieces struck from a new die.

REVERSE

Full strike on eagle's breast feathers. Usually complete on wings as well. May lack in pinfeather detail.

M.S. 64

OBVERSE

Bagmarks and blemishes are miniscule and certainly not in obvious places such as face, neck, leg, shield. Usually much stronger strike, and details are improved over M.S. 63. Still a bit short of 65. Eye appeal is somewhat improved over the M.S. 63 grade.

REVERSE

Much improved. Usually would grade a 65 unless miniscule bagmarks prevent it.

M.S. 63

OBVERSE

Much better than M.S. 60 in every respect. Many less bagmarks. Better strike. Evenly toned, but will still lack in sharpness of strike in head, shield, knee and chain mail.

REVERSE

Eagle's breast much improved from M.S. 60. But will have a few bagmarks. Should be evenly toned—but not always.

M.S. 60

OBVERSE

A very typical (new coin). Strictly uncirculated, with no trace of wear at all. Usually many bag nicks, scrapes, spots, and usually has undesirable toning—mottled or dull. Most likely head lacks in details as well as other areas such as shield, knee, toes, and gown. Also Liberty's right breast. Little or no eye appeal.

REVERSE

Eagle's breast feathers usually weak as well as left wing feathers. Beak and head will usually be weak also. May be uneven toning, with nicks and/or bagmarks.

AU—ALMOST UNCIRCULATED, 55

OBVERSE

Just a trace of wear or rub on the highest points—inner shield, right knee, breast and chain mail covering. Looks uncirculated to the untrained eye. About 80-90% mint luster.

REVERSE

Light wear or rub on eagle's breast and edges of wings. 80-90% mint luster.

AU—ALMOST UNCIRCULATED, 50

OBVERSE

Progressed wear from the 55 description. Rub usually means wear at this point and the right knee, breast and mail covering will have a light brown or amber color on these points (unless coin has been cleaned). About 50-60% mint luster remains.

REVERSE

Worn spots show on center of breast feathers as well as wings. Tail feathers show some wear in this grade as well.

XF—EXTRA FINE, 45

OBVERSE

Right leg and knee begin to show light wear in spots. Gown lines crossing Liberty's thigh are clearly visible. Good detail in shield, but a few horizontal lines may be worn flat. Chain mail over left breast will be slightly worn (only a few links will be worn together), but breast will still be rounded—except the very point.

REVERSE

Eagle's right wing will show much wear but CAN-NOT be smooth. Most of tail feathers are still visible. (Full on stronger strikes such as '30-P, '29-P and '26-P.)

XF—EXTRA FINE, 40

OBVERSE

Right leg worn about half way from calf to thigh. Breast shows definite wear. Practically all gown lines worn away. Shield details are there except vertical and horizontal lines are worn away. Liberty's left breast is about 1/3 worn down.

REVERSE

Eagle's right wing worn nearly smooth. Also about 1/2 to 2/3 of tail feathers are still visible. Breast feathers are worn about 1/2 away as well. Should expect 20-30% mint luster if coin is not toned.

VF—VERY FINE, 30

OBVERSE

Considerable wear on shield, leg, breast. Right leg worn from ankle to thigh. But, should still be rounded some. Some gown lines show on Liberty's torso. About 1/2 of chain mail over Liberty's breasts shows.

REVERSE

Eagle's leg and breast are worn, but still separated. Major details show, but eagle's edge of right wing is worn flat. Top tail feathers are complete, as is rim.

F - FINE, 15

OBVERSE

Only major outlines show. Most gown lines worn away except those closest to Liberty's body and right leg. Toes are flat. Some chain mail may show. Date remains strong on Ty. 3 in this grade because of the recessed date (1925-30).

REVERSE

Full rim. All letters clear and separated from the rim. Eagle's breast worn smooth. About 1/2 of wing feathers will show, with the spots worn away completely.

VG - VERY GOOD, 8

OBVERSE

Most details worn smooth. Entire design is weak, including letters. About 1/2 of drapery lines show across Liberty's bust and waist, but not complete. Full rim and clear date.

REVERSE

Flight feathers at tips of wings still separated. About 1/3 or less of the feathers on eagle's wings show. Claws are still separated. The letters and rim are still separated as well.

G—GOOD, 4

OBVERSE

Very little detail remains. Entire design virtually gone, except for major details. "In God we trust" very weak. Date is still complete. Rim slightly worn into letters. Two bottom stars (right and left sides) worn away.

REVERSE

Eagle worn flat. Outlined only. Letters worn into rim. Stars and letters worn flat as well.

AG—ABOUT GOOD, 3*

OBVERSE

Miss Liberty is outlined, but nearly all details worn away. Legend readable but about 1/2 worn away. Rim worn into tops of letters. Date weak. Maybe partially worn away, but should be discernible.

Your author does not recommend this grade as a collector's item.

Chapter 8

RARE DISCOVERIES IN STANDING LIBERTY QUARTERS

•

STRANGE & UNUSUAL STANDING LIBERTY QUARTERS

A Rare Find In Standing Liberty Quarters

This article originally appeared in Coin World, July 11, 1984.

I GUESS YOU NEVER know what you'll find in Dayton, Ohio. Pictured above is a coin that I purchased just last Fall (1983) in Dayton, Ohio, and I must admit the scarcity and rarity of this can only be appreciated by those of us who are Standing Liberty Quarter enthusiasts. I have handled, purchased, sold and traded a lot of Standing Liberty Quarter errors since (as most every one who will take the time to read this article knows) I have spent an awful, awful lot of research time, effort, money, etc., etc., on the Standing Liberty Quarter series and, of course, authored a book on Standing Liberty Quarters. The above pictured Standing Liberty Quarter is, by and large, the furthest off-center I have ever seen.

This particular thing could happen only in a large mintage year; maybe a little sloppy in operation, but it certainly was the era when people were conscientious about their work performed...whether in a factory, in an office, on a farm, or wherever, as this is virtually nonexistent and was commented as such by other authors. In my own book, I commented how scarce this particular error (well, any errors) in the Standing Liberty Quarter series are, because they were produced in a very conscientious time in our society.

To give you a general idea of how other people think the Standing Liberty Quarter errors are scarce, at the A.N.A. in 1979 in St. Louis, Mo., the first place to exhibitors was given to a man who had an exhibit of six Standing Liberty Quarter errors. I am proud to say that I own most of those pieces today—none of which would even approach the scarcity of this particular piece. I have seen errors and owned a good many errors in Standing Liberty Quarters, and admittedly, this is my pride and joy.

I don't quite rate it as rare as I do the Full Head 1916 or the overdate, or even the 1919-D for that matter, but I do admit that it is a very unusual piece—something that has been sought by several Standing Liberty Quarter enthusiasts. It has been believed by many that there was no piece like this in existence. That conscientiousness of the workers of the mint in this era of time was such that all coins such as this were thrown back in the hopper and remelted. I could name several people in this wonderful hobby that we call numismatics that say things such as this could not happen at this time in our society.

For those that may not be fully familiar with the minting process or the odds against something like this happening, let me paint you a picture, verbally. The striking process of this and any other coin is as follows: the dies have a collar that guides the punching operation and guides the die onto the surface of the coin. In our very early coinage, of course, these collars were not used and consequently, you find a lot of coins that were struck off-center, rotated dies, etc., etc., that make up so many of the varieties—especially in the large cents and the bust halves (two just off the top of my head) that were struck without collars. But the collar, or guide let's call it, was initiated in about the 1850 era and, therefore, there are far less coins off-center since 1850 as there were in previous years.

Striking hubs for obverse and reverse have one guide, or collar, that guides the striking die onto the surface of the blank disc that is about to receive the image of the coin. Any coin struck out of collar could be varying amounts off-center. Whenever the clearance between the shaft and the die and the collar fills with scrap metal, this causes the die to stick inside the collar when the die is in the "up" position. Then, when the die drops down, it pulls the collar down. The end result: the die and collar combination forms a flat surface when the blank is fed in. It could land anywhere and is struck in whatever position it lands in. The collar rides up with the hammer die and strikes the coin off-center wherever it happens to land after having been fed into the dies by the feeder.

The coin is then produced and the obverse and reverse land wherever it will—almost never centered on that planchet.

Most collectors, or at least the avid ones, that have been around the numismatic field for any length of time (and especially if they specialize in one series or another) have a few of their particular interest series struck out of collar, off center, or double struck, or a brockage and so forth.

So you can readily see why a coin struck this far off-center is a very unusual piece, and making a coin in this era of time a very scarce coin because they were, as I said before, very conscientious people at this time in our society.

Admittedly, some of our modern day coinage is very readily available both double and sometimes even triple struck, because the processes used today are "hurry up and get it done" or a little less scrutiny in quality control, and unfortunately the conscientiousness of our society concerning their work habits is not in our present day what it was in the 1920 era.

I guess everything has a price tag and it wouldn't be fair to say as much as I've said about this coin without giving you an estimation of its value. As I said, any errors in Standing Liberty Quarters are very, very rare and this being the only one that is this far off-center that yours truly has seen in 30 years or so in the numismatic world, and collecting and admiring Standing Liberty Quarters. This is the first either heard of, or that I've seen—or that anyone else I've talked to has ever seen that is this far off-center. So the value that I would place on this coin would be several thousand dollars, and I must add, very quickly that even at that, it is not for sale. It's just some thing that I thought I should say about the value of the piece. When you have a unique piece, or virtually unique, then what kind of a price structure do you use on a coin. That's kind of like a 1917 matte proof Standing Liberty Quarter. There were six pieces only made of that. How could you possibly establish what one piece is worth, and assuming that there are very few of them left, as with something like this off-center quarter. If there are very few pieces that ever change hands, there is certainly no way to establish an honest value numismatically speaking.

I will say, just for the record, that I have refused several thousand dollars for this coin, and would be interested in seeing and perhaps purchasing any coins that anywhere near approach this amount of off-center in the Standing Liberty Quarter series. I would invite any communication concerning Standing Liberty Quarter errors—large or small.

J. H. Cline
LM ANA #547

Standing Liberty Quarters Rare Discoveries

This article originally appeared in Coin World in September, 1983

Possibly a unique error coin owned by a mid-west collector is this Standing Liberty quarter struck on a cent planchet. Author J.H. Cline theorizes that the coin could have been illicitly struck by a worker at the Mint.

With everyone searching, looking and scanning their pocket change, current coinage by modern production methods keeps most people busy just staying abreast of modern errors since so many mis-struck coins appear in circulation.

But now and then, a real numismatic rarity surfaces. Something that is rare and genuinely Mint-made—a major error.

Having researched Standing Liberty quarters as much as, or more than, anyone in the hobby, I can say with absolute authority that the Standing Liberty quarter series has less errors—overstrikes, double strikes, off-center strikes, clips and clashed dies—than any other series.

You rarely see Mint errors advertised for sale in any of the numismatic publications. To find them, you almost have to know someone, or do a lot of looking and research for yourself.

An exhibit at the 1979 American Numismatic Association convention in St. Louis won first place in the error category with only six coins (one was a broken planchet). The rarity of mis-struck Standing quarters is appreciated by the hobby, including ANA judges who are certified, knowledgeable and unbiased numismatic experts.

To quote from my book, Standing Liberty Quarters, "This is one of the [least mis-struck] series of the entire U.S. coinage; all in all, almost an errorless era of coins."

Since the release of my book in 1976, I have intensified my efforts in locating errors in the Standing Liberty quarter series and could count on two hands, with fingers left over, the number I have found and could buy, including the ANA display I bought in 1979.

Recently, at the Indiana State Numismatic Association's annual convention, noted collector and dealer a mid-west collector walked up to me on the bourse floor and said, "Jay, look what I found in the bottom of my lock-box" He handed me a 1928 Standing Liberty quarter struck on a Lincoln cent planchet, and a 1929-S double-struck piece—both grading nearly About Uncirculated.

I asked if he remembered where he got the coins. He said he forgot the origins of the 1929-S double-struck coin, but the one struck on the Lincoln cent planchet he purchased for a few hundred dollars at the 1958 ANA convention in Los Angeles.

He said he promptly took it over to a well-known Philadelphia dealer who did not make the right offer, so he took the coin home, put it in his lock-box and three weeks ago took it out for the first time since. He said the uniqueness of this coin should have placed it at a higher value, so he kept it. And I am sure glad he did.

The uniqueness of this coin can be fully appreciated by only a handful of collectors. As far as I know, this is the only Standing Liberty quarter struck on a Lincoln cent planchet. Just in the past two weeks, I have talked to several error specialists and all are of the same mind—this is the only one known to exist. Two of the people I talked to identified him by name. None had ever heard of this error happening before.

The distance separating minting facilities for silver, gold and copper coinage, and other dividers which keep them apart, should have kept this error from ever happening; or at least from getting out of the Mint.

There are two schools of thought as to how this could have happened. The first is strictly coincidence. From some reason, a cent planchet made its way to the quarter stamping machine. Maybe the job-setter who installed the new dies used the blank as a set-up piece because of the softness of copper.

The second theory (and the one I adhere to) is that a workman in the Lincoln cent department and a workman in the quarter department got together and agreed to strike each other wrong planchet coins.

Maybe none of these theories are correct. Could be the error fell out of the wild blue yonder and is the only one of its kind. I would be interested to learn just how many more exist, if any.

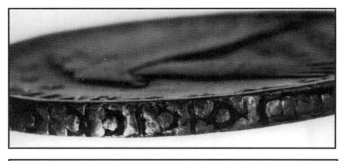

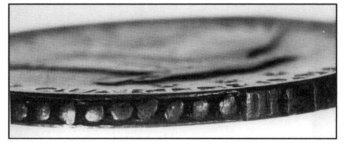

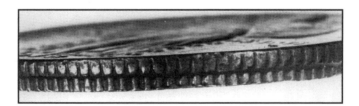

The above three Standing Liberty Quarters (all dated 1920) have some strange rims. Rolled and tooled – very professional looking; however all were altered outside the U.S. Mint. All Standing Liberty Quarters have standard milling by U.S. Mint standards.

This is the only railroad rim Standing Liberty Quarter I have ever seen to date.

This coin has re-engraved hair and olive leaves at ear and horizontal hair at bottom half of hair style. This coin was offered by one of the major auction houses in a set. After I pointed out the re-engraving to them, they quickly removed it from the set prior to the sale.

A 1924 Standing Liberty Quarter that was struck with a broken die. Quite a severe broken die and it was most likely discarded or broke away completely on the next few strikes.

Some very pronounced clash marks from the obverse which is of course the profile of Miss Liberty. Struck a bit too hard and causes her profile to come through to the reverse of the coin.

All errors of Standing Liberty Quarters large or small are rare. This was the era of conscientious workers at the Mints and most errors were returned to the hopper for melting. I have not seen another quite like this one.

Small cud on the opposite side from the teardrop: 1920-S, 26-S & 28-S.

This is an added mintmark on a BU coin. Also a different die break than other 1924-S — it might be an added mintmark on a 1924-D??? The striking traits are that of the 1924-D (that is the top half of the date is very weak).

Chapter 9

PROGRESS
ANALYSIS

The following pages are given to compare what Standing Liberty Quarters have done over the last 45 years. We have tried to give you some of the available information on the Standing Liberty Quarter from 1951 through 1995. All prices are from R.S. Yeoman's, "A Guide Book of United States Coins":

STANDING LIBERTY QUARTERS: 1951-52

	FINE	UNC.		FINE	UNC.
Type 1			1923	1.25	5.00
			1923-S	10.00	30.00
1916	$35.00	$90.00	1924	1.25	4.50
1917 Type I	1.00	2.75	1924-D	1.50	4.00
1917-D Type 1	2.00	11.50	1924-S	2.50	15.00
1917-S Type 1	2.50	12.50			
			Type 3		
Type 2				FINE	UNC.
	FINE	UNC.	1925	1.00	3.75
1917 Type 2	1.75	6.00	1926	.75	4.00
1917-D Type 2	3.00	20.00	1926-D	.75	2.00
1917-S Type 2	2.75	25.00	1926-S	4.00	40.00
1918	2.00	12.50	1927	.75	6.00
1918-D	2.50	17.50	1927-D	1.00	3.25
1918-S	2.00	16.00	1927-S	6.00	75.00
1918-S over 7	50 00	150.00	1928	.75	5.00
1919	2.50	14.00	1928-D	.50	2.00
1919-D	4.50	20.00	1928-S	75	5 00
1919-S	7.50	65.00	1929	.60	2.50
1920	1.25	5.00	1929-D	.75	3.00
1920-D	5.00	27.50	1929-S	.75	3.00
1920-S	2.50	15.00	1930	.60	2.50
1921	10.00	50.00	1930-S	.75	3.50

QUOTES WITHOUT COMMENT

The Numismatist was quoting prices brought by Stack's Auction at Detroit (circa 1940). They stated that an Isabella quarter sold for $15.00. It must have been struck in Platinum (Editor's note: this was the last lot of the sale and four gold dollars and a $3 gold piece was thrown in with the Isabella—not to mention Joe Stack's necktie!).

STANDING LIBERTY QUARTERS: 1958

Variety 1

	GOOD	FINE	UNC.
1916	$57.50	$85.00	$180.00
1917 Variety 1 .50	2.25	6.50	
1917-D" "	1.50	4.00	16.00
1917-S" "	2.50	7.50	22.50

Variety 2

	GOOD	FINE	UNC.
1917	1.25	4.00	10.00
1917-D	2.50	7.50	30.00
1917-S	2.50	7.50	35.00
1918	1.35	4.50	40.00
1918-D	2.25	6.00	35.00
1918-S	1.35	4.50	25.00
1918-S over7	40.00	90.00	325.00
1919	2.00	5.50	27.50
1919-D	6.00	14.00	45.00
1919-S	8.50	22.50	125.00
1920	.75	2.50	9.50
1920-D	5 00	11.00	55 00
1920-S	1.75	5.00	25.00
1921	9.00	20.00	95.00

	GOOD	FINE	UNC.
1923	.75	2.50	7.50
1923-S	15.00	32.50	80.00
1924	.60	2.00	8.50
1924-D	2.00	4.00	8.00
1924-S	3.50	8.50	32.50
1925		1.75	7.00
1926		1.50	8.00
1926-D		1.50	5.00
1926-S	1.00	14.00	75.00
1927		1.50	9.00
1927-D	.50	1.75	6.00
1927-S	1.00	15.00	200.00
1928		1.50	9.00
1928-D		1.00	5.00
1928-S	.50	1.50	7.50
1929		1.00	5.00
1929-D		1.50	6.50
1929-S		1.50	6.50
1930		1.00	4.50
1930-S		1.50	7.50

STANDING LIBERTY QUARTERS: 1962

Variety 1

	GOOD	FINE	EX. FINE	UNC.
1916	$100.00	175.00	240.00	400.00
1917	2.00	4.00	7.50	12.50
1917-D	2.50	6.50	16.00	30.00
1917-S	3.00	8.50	16.00	35.00

Variety 2

	GOOD	FINE	EX. FINE	UNC.
1917	1.75	5.00	10.00	16.00
1917-D	4.00	11.00	22.50	45.00
1917-S	4.00	11.00	22.50	45.00
1918	2.25	7.00	22.50	42.50
1918-D	3.50	8.00	25.00	52.50
1918-S	2.25	7.00	17.50	39.00
1918-S over 7				
	75.00	185.00	350.00	900.00
1919	3.00	7.00	22.00	37.50
1919-D	12.00	30.00	70.00	120.00
1919-S	18.00	45.00	90.00	190.00
1920	1.50	3.50	6.50	13.00
1920-D	7.00	16.00	40.00	72.50
1920-S	3.50	7.50	17.50	45.00

	GOOD	FINE	EX. FINE	UNC.
1921	11.00	24.00	55.00	110.00
1923	1.50	3.50	6.00	11.50
1923-S	20.00	42.50	85.00	150.00
1924	1.50	3.50	6.00	11.50
1924-D	3.50	5.50	9.00	15.00
1924-S	4.00	9.00	20.00	50.00
1925		2.50	5.00	11.00
1926		2.50	5.00	11.00
1926-D		2.50	3.50	8.50
1926-S	3.00	10.00	50.00	100.00
1927		2.00	4.00	13.00
1927-D		2.00	5.00	15.00
1927-S	5.00	13.50	95.00	390.00
1928		1.50	4.50	12.50
1928-D		1.50	4.50	10.00
1928-S		1.50	4.50	11.00
1929		1.50	4.50	9.50
1929-D		1.50	4.50	11.00
1929-S		1.50	4.50	11.00
1930		1.50	4.50	8.50
1930-S		1.50	4.50	11.00

Variety 1

	QUAN. MINTED	GOOD	V.G.	FINE	E.F.	UNC.
1916	52,000	225.00	325.00	425.00	650.00	950.00
1917	8,792,000	2.75	3.75	5.50	13.50	45.50
1917-D	1,509,200	5.25	7.00	10.00	20.00	55.00
1917-S	1,952,000	5.25	7.00	10.00	22.50	65.00

Variety 2

	QUAN. MINTED	GOOD	V.G.	FINE	E.F.	UNC.
1917	13,880,000	3.00	4.25	7.25	15.50	37.50
1917-D	6,224,400	6.50	11.00	14.00	27.50	70.00
1917-S	5,552,000	8.00	12.50	16.50	30.00	72.50
1918	14,240,000	3.25	5.00	8.00	25.00	57.50
1918-D	7,380,000	6.50	9.50	13.00	30.00	77.50
1918-S (Normal Date)	11,072,000	3.75	5.75	9.00	23.00	65.00
1918-S 8 Over 7	Unknown		280.00	440.00	850.00	2,900.00
1919	11,324,000	4.00	5.75	9.00	24.00	55.00
1919-D	1,944,000	25.00	32.50	47.50	110.00	285.00
1919-S	1,836,000	27.00	36.50	55.00	115.00	335.00
1920	27,860,000	3.00	4.00	5.50	11.00	35.00
1920-D	3,586,400	9.00	14.00	22.00	50.00	135.00
1920-S	6,380,000	6.50	9.50	13.00	27.50	75.00
1921	1,916,000	21.00	28.50	42.50	80.00	250.00
1923	9,716,000	2.00	3.50	5.25	11.00	32.50
1923-S	1,360,000	37.50	50.00	65.00	115.00	250.00
1924	10,920,000	2.00	3.50	5.25	11.00	37.50
1924-D	3,112,000	7.50	10.00	12.50	22.50	50.00
1924-S	2,860,000	8.50	12.00	17.50	35.00	100.00
1925	12,280,000		.75	2.75	6.00	32.50
1926	11,316,000		.75	2.75	6.00	30.00
1926-D	1,716,000		1.00	3.00	7.00	30.00
1926-S	2,700,000	2.25	3.50	6.50	47.50	160.00
1927	11,912,000		.75	2.25	6.00	35.00
1927-D	976,400	2.00	3.25	5.50	13.00	72.50
1927-S	396,000	5.00	7.25	15.00	130.00	725.00
1928	6,336,000		.65	2.00	5.50	30.00
1928-D	1,627,600		.75	2.25	6.50	32.50
1928-S	2,644,000		.75	2.00	6.00	32.50
1929	11,140,000		.65	1.85	4.75	30.00
1929-D	1,358,000		.75	2.00	6.00	45.00
1929-S	1,764,000		.75	2.00	5.50	35.00
1930	5,632,000		.65	1.85	4.75	30.00
1930-S	1,556,000		.75	2.00	5.25	35.00

Variety 1

	QUAN. MINTED	GOOD	V.G.	FINE	V.F.	E.F.	UNC.
1916	52,000	250.00	325.00	410.00	490.00	575.00	875.00
1917	8,792,000	3.50	4.75	6.75	10.25	17.50	50.00
1917-D	1,509,200	5.75	7.75	11.00	16.00	22.50	65.00
1917-S	1,952,000	5.75	7.75	11.00	16.00	22.50	70.00

Variety 2

	QUAN. MINTED	GOOD	V.G.	FINE	V.F.	E.F.	UNC.
1917	13,880,000	3.50	5.00	7.50	11.00	17.50	40.00
1917-D	6,224,400	7.50	12.00	16.50	21.00	30.00	70.00
1917-S	5,552,000	10.00	14.00	18.00	25.00	35.00	72.50
1918	14,240,000	4.00	6.00	10.00	15.00	25.00	57.50
1918-D	7,380,000	7.50	10.50	15.00	22.50	30.00	75.00
1918-S (Normal Date)	11,072,000	4.00	6.00	10.00	15.00	25.00	65.00
1918-S 8 Over7	Unknown		300.00	475.00	625.00	900.00	3,250.00
1919	11,324,000	5.00	6.75	10.00	15.00	25.00	55.00
1919-D	1,944,000	25.00	32.50	47.50	65.00	115.00	290.00
1919-S	1,836,000	27.50	37.50	50.00	70.00	125.00	325.00
1920	27,860,000	3.50	4.50	6.00	8.50	12.00	37.50
1920-D	3,586,400	10.00	15.00	22.50	30.00	55.00	130.00
1920-S	6,380,000	7.00	9.50	13.00	18.50	28.00	75.00
1921	1,916,000	22.50	30.00	45.00	62.50	90.00	150.00
1923	9,716,000	2.50	4.00	6.00	8.50	12.00	35.00
1923-S	1,360,000	37.50	50.00	65.00	85.00	110.00	160.00
1924	10,920,000	2.50	4.00	6.00	8.50	12.00	37.50
1924-D	3,112,000	8.50	12.00	14.00	19.00	25.00	52.50
1924-S	2,860,000	9.50	12.50	18.00	25.00	35.00	97.50

Recessed Date Style 1925-1930

	QUAN. MINTED	GOOD	V.G.	FINE	V.F.	E.F.	UNC.
1925	12,280,000	.65	1.00	2.75	4.00	7.50	32.50
1926	11,316,000	.65	1.00	2.75	4.00	7.50	32.50
1926-D	1,716,000	.85	1.25	3.50	5.00	8.50	35.00
1926-S	2,700,000	2.25	3.50	6.50	18.50	45.00	160.00
1927	11,912,000	.65	1.00	2.50	3.75	7.00	35.00
1927-D	976,400	2.25	3.50	6.00	9.50	17.50	80.00
1927-S	396,000	5.00	7.50	15.00	75.00	140.00	700.00
1928	6,336,000	.65	1.00	2.25	3.50	6.75	34.00
1928-D	1,627,600	.65	1.00	2.75	3.75	7.50	35.00
1928-S	2,644,000	.65	1.00	2.75	3.75	7.50	35.00
1929	11,140,000	.60	.90	1.75	3.00	7.00	35.00
1929-D	1,358,000	.60	1.00	2.25	3.50	7.50	45.00
1929-S	1,764,000	.60	1.00	2.25	3.50	7.50	40.00
1930	5,632,000	.60	1.00	2.25	3.50	7.00	32.50
1930-S	1,556,000	.60	1.00	2.25	3.50	7.50	40.00

Variety 1

	QUAN. MINTED	GOOD	V.G.	FINE	V.F.	E.F.	UNC.
1916	52,000	335.00	425.00	575.00	775.00	975.00	1,750.00
1917	8,792,000	7.50	9.00	12.00	20.00	50.00	250.00
1917-D	1,509,200	8.00	9.50	13.00	24.00	60.00	260.00
1917-S	1,952,000	8.00	9.50	13.00	24.00	60.00	275.00

Variety 2

	QUAN. MINTED	GOOD	V.G.	FINE	V.F.	E.F.	UNC.
1917	13,880,000	6.00	8.00	11.50	17.00	30.00	130.00
1917-D	6,224,400	11.00	13.00	20.00	25.00	37.50	145.00
1917-S	5,552,000	12.50	16.00	22.50	27.50	40.00	145.00
1918	14,240,000	6.00	8.00	11.50	16.00	35.00	125.00
1918-D	7,380,000	10.50	12.00	16.00	24.00	40.00	150.00
1918-S (Normal Date)	11,072,000	6.00	8.00	11.50	18.00	35.00	140.00
1918-S 8 Over7	Unknown	235.00	340.00	550.00	725.00	1,150.00	6,000.00
1919	11,324,000	9.50	12.00	17.00	24.00	34.00	130.00
1919-D	1,944,000	28.00	36.00	50.00	65.00	115.00	385.00
1919-S	1,836,000	35.00	45.00	60.00	75.00	125.00	390.00
1920	27,860,000	4.25	5.50	8.00	10.00	22.00	125.00
1920-D	3,586,400	13.00	17.00	22.00	32.00	60.00	175.00
1920-S	6,380,000	8.50	11.50	14.00	21.00	30.00	150.00
1921	1,916,000	25.00	35.00	50.00	65.00	90.00	375.00
1923	9,716,000	4.00	5.00	7.00	9.00	18.00	125.00
1923-S	1,360,000	47.50	58.00	75.00	100.00	135.00	425.00
1924	10,920,000	4.00	5.00	7.00	10.00	20.00	125.00
1924-D	3,112,000	13.00	18.00	21.00	28.00	37.50	135.00
1924-S	2,860,000	10.00	12.00	16.00	27.00	35.00	160.00

Recessed Date Style 1925-1930

	QUAN. MINTED	GOOD	V.G.	FINE	V.F.	E.F.	UNC.
1925	12,280,000	1.50	2.00	3.00	7.00	20.00	115.00
1926	11,316,000	1.50	2.00	3.00	7.00	20.00	115.00
1926-D	1,716,000	2.00	3.50	6.00	12.50	27.00	115.00
1926-S	2,700,000	2.00	3.00	5.00	10.00	30.00	225.00
1927	11,912,000	1.50	2.00	3.00	7.00	20.00	100.00
1927-D	976,400	2.25	4.00	8.50	15.00	31.00	125.00
1927-S	396,000	5.00	7.50	15.00	50.00	140.00	1,000.00
1928	6,336,000	1.50	2.00	3.00	7.00	20.00	100.00
1928-D	1,627,600	1.50	2.00	3.00	7.00	21.00	100.00
1928-S	2,644,000	1.50	2.00	3.00	7.00	20.00	100.00
1929	11,140,000	1.50	2.00	3.00	7.00	20.00	100.00
1929-D	1,358,000	1.75	2.25	3.25	7.50	22.50	125.00
1929-S	1,764,000	1.50	2.00	3.00	7.00	20.00	100.00
1930	5,632,000	1.50	2.00	3.00	7.00	20.00	100.00
1930-S	1,556,000	1.50	2.00	3.00	7.00	20.00	100.00

Variety 1

	QUAN. MINTED	GOOD	V.G.	FINE	V.F.	E.F.	UNC.
1916	52,000	1,100.00	1,400.00	1,700.00	2,000.00	2,500.00	4,500.00
1917	8,792,000	9.00	12.00	16.00	30.00	60.00	250.00
1917-D	1,509,200	12.00	16.00	23.00	60.00	110.00	325.00
1917-S	1,952,000	12.00	16.00	23.00	60.00	110.00	350.00

Variety 2

	QUAN. MINTED	GOOD	V.G.	FINE	V.F.	E.F.	UNC.
1917	13,880,000	10.00	14.00	18.00	25.00	40.00	200.00
1917-D	6,224,400	20.00	25.00	45.00	65.00	110.00	350.00
1917-S	5,552,000	18.00	23.00	32.00	50.00	85.00	350.00
1918	14,240,000	12.00	16.00	25.00	35.00	55.00	235.00
1918-D	7,380,000	22.00	26.00	40.00	60.00	95.00	385.00
1918-S (Normal Date)	11,072,000	12.00	16.00	22.50	30.00	50.00	235.00
1918-S 8 Over7	Unknown	1,000.00	1,400.00	1,800.00	2,500.00	3,750.00	15,000.00
1919	11,324,000	28.00	32.00	40.00	50.00	75.00	210.00
1919-D	1,944,000	45.00	70.00	100.00	140.00	240.00	925.00
1919-S	1,836,000	45.00	65.00	95.00	130.00	220.00	850.00
1920	27,860,000	10.00	15.00	18.00	22.50	37.50	200.00
1920-D	3,586,400	25.00	35.00	50.00	75.00	125.00	400.00
1920-S	6,380,000	12.50	18.00	24.00	30.00	50.00	235.00
1921	1,916,000	50.00	80.00	125.00	160.00	250.00	725.00
1923	9,716,000	10.00	15.00	19.00	25.00	40.00	235.00
1923-S	1,360,000	100.00	150.00	210.00	275.00	400.00	800.00
1924	10,920,000	10.00	15.00	19.00	25.00	40.00	235.00
1924-D	3,112,000	25.00	30.00	40.00	60.00	90.00	240.00
1924-S	2,860,000	15.00	18.00	25.00	30.00	45.00	325.00

Recessed Date Style 1925-1930

	QUAN. MINTED	GOOD	V.G.	FINE	V.F.	E.F.	UNC.
1925	12,280,000	2.75	3.50	9.00	15.00	25.00	185.00
1926	11,316,000	2.75	3.50	9.00	15.00	25.00	185.00
1926-D	1,716,000	7.00	7.50	12.00	19.00	40.00	185.00
1926-S	2,700,000	2.75	3.50	11.00	19.00	55.00	375.00
1927	11,912,000	2.75	3.50	9.00	15.00	25.00	185.00
1927-D	976,400	8.00	10.00	15.00	30.00	60.00	275.00
1927-S	396,000	12.00	22.00	65.00	160.00	600.00	2,500.00
1928	6,336,000	2.75	3.50	9.00	15.00	25.00	185.00
1928-D	1,627,600	5.00	8.00	12.00	18.00	38.00	200.00
1928-S	2,644,000	4.00	6.00	10.00	16.00	30.00	200.00
1929	11,140,000	2.75	3.50	9.00	15.00	25.00	185.00
1929-D	1,358,000	5.00	8.00	12.00	18.00	32.00	200.00
1929-S	1,764,000	4.00	6.00	10.00	16.00	30.00	200.00
1930	5,632,000	2.75	3.50	9.00	15.00	25.00	185.00
1930-S	1,556,000	2.75	3.50	9.00	15.00	28.00	185.00

Variety 1

	QUAN. MINTED	GOOD	V.G.	FINE	V.F.	E.F.	UNC.
1916	52,000	1,000.00	1,200.00	1,500.00	1,800.00	2,200.00	4,300.00
1917	8,792,000	9.00	12.00	15.00	30.00	60.00	550.00
1917-D	1,509,200	13.00	17.00	24.00	55.00	100.00	600.00
1917-S	1,952,000	12.00	16.00	23.00	50.00	90.00	625.00

Variety 2

	QUAN. MINTED	GOOD	V.G.	FINE	V.F.	E.F.	UNC.
1917	13,880,000	10.00	14.00	18.00	25.00	40.00	350.00
1917-D	6,224,400	20.00	25.00	45.00	65.00	100.00	425.00
1917-S	5,552,000	18.00	23.00	32.00	50.00	80.00	450.00
1918	14,240,000	13.00	17.00	25.00	35.00	55.00	400.00
1918-D	7,380,000	22.00	26.00	40.00	60.00	95.00	450.00
1918-S (Normal Date)	11,072,000	13.00	17.00	22.50	30.00	50.00	400.00
1918-S 8 Over7	Unknown	1,000.00	1,300.00	1,700.00	2,200.00	3,250.00	14,000.00
1919	11,324,000	27.00	32.00	40.00	50.00	75.00	400.00
1919-D	1,944,000	45.00	70.00	100.00	140.00	240.00	950.00
1919-S	1,836,000	45.00	65.00	95.00	130.00	220.00	900.00
1920	27,860,000	12.00	15.00	18.00	22.50	37.50	350.00
1920-D	3,586,400	25.00	35.00	50.00	75.00	125.00	450.00
1920-S	6,380,000	13.00	18.00	24.00	30.00	50.00	400.00
1921	1,916,000	50.00	80.00	125.00	160.00	250.00	750.00
1923	9,716,000	12.00	15.00	19.00	25.00	40.00	350.00
1923-S	1,360,000	100.00	150.00	210.00	275.00	400.00	800.00
1924	10,920,000	11.00	15.00	19.00	25.00	40.00	350.00
1924-D	3,112,000	25.00	30.00	40.00	60.00	90.00	375.00
1924-S	2,860,000	15.00	18.00	25.00	30.00	45.00	400.00

Recessed Date Style 1925-1930

	QUAN. MINTED	GOOD	V.G.	FINE	V.F.	E.F.	UNC.
1925	12,280,000	2.75	3.50	7.00	15.00	25.00	300.00
1926	11,316,000	2.75	3.50	7.00	15.00	25.00	300.00
1926-D	1,716,000	7.00	7.50	12.00	19.00	40.00	300.00
1926-S	2,700,000	2.75	3.50	11.00	19.00	55.00	425.00
1927	11,912,000	2.75	3.50	7.00	15.00	25.00	300.00
1927-D	976,400	8.00	10.00	15.00	30.00	60.00	375.00
1927-S	396,000	12.00	22.00	65.00	160.00	600.00	2,200.00
1928	6,336,000	2.75	3.50	7.00	15.00	25.00	300.00
1928-D	1,627,600	5.00	8.00	12.00	18.00	38.00	325.00
1928-S	2,644,000	4.00	6.00	10.00	16.00	30.00	325.00
1929	11,140,000	2.75	3.50	7.00	15.00	25.00	300.00
1929-D	1,358,000	5.00	8.00	12.00	18.00	32.00	325.00
1929-S	1,764,000	4.00	6.00	10.00	16.00	30.00	300.00
1930	5,632,000	2.75	3.50	7.00	15.00	25.00	300.00
1930-S	1,556,000	2.75	3.50	7.00	15.00	28.00	300.00

Variety 1

	QUAN. MINTED	GOOD	V.G.	FINE	V.F.	E.F.	UNC.
1916	52,000	900.00	1,300.00	1,500.00	1,900.00	2,500.00	5,500.00
1917	8,792,000	8.00	10.00	15.00	28.00	60.00	300.00
1917-D	1,509,200	13.00	17.00	25.00	50.00	85.00	350.00
1917-S	1,952,000	15.00	18.00	25.00	50.00	130.00	350.00

Variety 2

	QUAN. MINTED	GOOD	V.G.	FINE	V.F.	E.F.	UNC.
1917	13,880,000	12.00	15.00	18.00	25.00	40.00	200.00
1917-D	6,224,400	18.00	25.00	45.00	60.00	85.00	250.00
1917-S	5,552,000	18.00	23.00	32.00	50.00	70.00	250.00
1918	14,240,000	13.00	17.00	20.00	30.00	45.00	200.00
1918-D	7,380,000	20.00	25.00	36.00	55.00	80.00	450.00
1918-S (Normal Date)	11,072,000	15.00	17.00	22.50	28.00	45.00	350.00
1918-S 8 Over7	Unknown	1,000.00	1,300.00	1,700.00	2,400.00	4,000.00	22,000.00
1919	11,324,000	20.00	30.00	40.00	45.00	60.00	200.00
1919-D	1,944,000	40.00	65.00	100.00	150.00	250.00	700.00
1919-S	1,836,000	40.00	60.00	95.00	170.00	335.00	900.00
1920	27,860,000	12.00	15.00	18.00	25.00	35.00	200.00
1920-D	3,586,400	20.00	30.00	50.00	70.00	100.00	450.00
1920-S	6,380,000	15.00	18.00	24.00	28.00	42.00	450.00
1921	1,916,000	55.00	85.00	120.00	160.00	235.00	725.00
1923	9,716,000	12.00	15.00	19.00	25.00	39.00	200.00
1923-S	1,360,000	95.00	140.00	175.00	230.00	340.00	750.00
1924	10,920,000	14.00	15.00	22.00	25.00	35.00	200.00
1924-D	3,112,000	20.00	30.00	40.00	60.00	80.00	220.00
1924-S	2,860,000	15.00	20.00	21.00	30.00	75.00	550.00

Recessed Date Style 1925-1930

	QUAN. MINTED	GOOD	V.G.	FINE	V.F.	E.F.	UNC.
1925	12,280,000	3.00	3.50	7.00	18.00	29.00	185.00
1926	11,316,000	3.00	3.50	7.00	18.00	29.00	185.00
1926-D	1,716,000	7.00	9.00	15.00	22.00	50.00	200.00
1926-S	2,700,000	3.00	5.00	11.00	21.00	90.00	612.00
1927	11,912,000	3.00	3.50	7.00	15.00	25.00	185.00
1927-D	976,400	5.00	8.00	12.00	25.00	75.00	220.00
1927-S	396,000	10.00	15.00	50.00	145.00	950.00	4,100.00
1928	6,336,000	3.00	3.50	7.00	15.00	29.00	200.00
1928-D	1,627,600	4.00	7.00	10.00	17.00	35.00	200.00
1928-S	2,644,000	4.00	5.00	8.00	17.00	31.00	200.00
1929	11,140,000	3.00	3.00	7.00	13.00	28.00	185.00
1929-D	1,358,000	5.00	8.00	10.00	16.00	35.00	200.00
1929-S	1,764,000	3.00	5.00	7.00	15.00	30.00	185.00
1930	5,632,000	3.00	3.50	7.00	15.00	28.00	185.00
1930-S	1,556,000	3.00	3.50	7.00	13.00	28.00	195.00

STANDING LIBERTY QUARTERS
PRICE STANDING JUNE 11, 1976

FULL HEAD

	PRICE	QUANTITY	PRICE RANK	QUAN. RANK
1918/17-S$	11,000.00	Unknown	1	1
1916-P	2,300.00	52,000	2	2
1927-S	1,300.00	396,000	3	3
1919-D	950.00	1,944,000	4	14
1919-S	835.00	1,836,000	5	12
1921-P	725.00	1,916,000	6	13
1923-S	725.00	1,360,000	7	6
1926-D	700.00	1,716,000	8	10
1924-D	560.00	3,112,000	9	19
1928-D	500.00	1,627,000	10	9
1929-D	500.00	1,358,000	11	5
1918-D	450.00	7,380,000	12	26
1920-D	450.00	3,586,400	13	20
1917-D (II)	400.00	6,224,400	14	23
1926-S	390.00	2,700,000	15	17
1924-S	360.00	2,860,000	16	18
1917-S (I)	345.00	1,952,000	17	15
1917-S (II)	345.00	5,552,000	18	21
1918-S	345.00	11,072,000	19	30
1920-S	345.00	6,380,000	20	25
1927-D	345.00	976,400	21	4
1917-D (I)	325.00	1,509,200	22	7
1918-P	325.00	12,240,000	23	35
1919-P	325.00	11,324,000	24	33
1917-P (II)	315.00	13,880,000	25	37
1917-P (I)	310.00	8,792,000	26	27
1923-P	310.00	9,716,000	27	29
1924-P	310.00	10,920,000	28	28
1926-P	310.00	11,316,000	29	32
1920-P	300.00	27,860,000	30	38
1928-P	300.00	6,336,000	31	24
1930-S	300.00	1,556,000	32	8
1927-P	290.00	11,912,000	33	34
1925-P	280.00	12,280,000	34	36
1928-S	280.00	2,644,000	35	16
1929-P	280.00	11,140,000	36	31
1929-S	280.00	1,764,000	37	11
1930-P	280.00	5,632,000	38	22

From: the *COIN DEALER newsletter* MONTHLY SUMMARY JUNE—1979:

STANDING LIBERTY QUARTERS

	CH. BU	MS-65	FULL HEAD CH. BU.	FULL HEAD MS-65
1916-P	2700.00	2950.00	4750.00	—
1917-P (I)	200.00	220.00	365.00	400.00
1917-D (I)	220.00	240.00	425.00	470.00
1917-S (I)	220.00	240.00	425.00	470.00
1917-P (II)	150.00	165.00	410.00	455.00
1917-D (II)	190.00	210.00	560.00	615.00
1917-S (II)	190.00	210.00	560.00	615.00
1918-P	160.00	175.00	475.00	525.00
1918-D	235.00	260.00	800.00	900.00
1918/17-S	6750.00	—	17,000.00	—
1918-S	180.00	200.00	3000 00	—
1919-P	150.00	165.00	475.00	525.00
1919-D	675.00	735.00	2700.00	—
1919-S	675.00	735.00	2600.00	—
1920-P	147.50	162.50	410.00	455.00
1920-D	245.00	270.00	860.00	—
1920-S	220.00	245.00	2000.00	—
1921-P	400.00	440.00	940.00	—
1923-P	150.00	165.00	550.00	600.00
1923-S	525.00	575.00	1250.00	—
1924-P	150.00	165.00	425.00	480.00
1924-D	150.00	165.00	1000.00	—
1924-S	200.00	220.00	925.00	—
1925-P	130.00	142.50	400.00	435.00
1926-P	130.00	142.50	390.00	425.00
1926-D	130.00	142.50	1750.00	—
1926-S	350.00	385.00	2750.00	—
1927-P	130.00	142.50	395.00	430.00
1927-D	160.00	175.00	535.00	590.00
1927-S	2700.00	—	5000.00	—
1928-P	135.00	147.50	500.00	550.00
1928-S	50.00	165.00	1300.00	—
1928-S	135.00	147.50	400.00	435.00
1929-P	130.00	142.50	390.00	425.00
1929-D	150.00	165.00	1450.00	—
1929-S	130.00	142.50	400.00	435.00
1930-P	130.00	142.50	390.00	425.00
1930-S	135.00	147.50	410.00	450.00

From: the *COIN DEALER newsletter* MONTHLY SUMMARY JUNE—1982:

STANDING LIBERTY QUARTERS

	MS-65 BID	MS-65 ASK	FULL HEAD MS-65 BID	FULL HEAD MS-65 ASK		MS-65 BID	MS-65 ASK	FULL HEAD MS-65 BID	FULL HEAD MS-65 ASK
1916-P	4250.00	4750.00	9000.00	10,000.00	1923-S	1600.00	1775.00	4500.00	5000.00
1917-P (I)	425.00	470.00	1000.00	1125.00	1924-P	525.00	585.00	2250.00	2500.00
1917-D (I)	540.00	600.00	1300.00	1450.00	1924-D	500.00	560.00	2700.00	3000.00
1917-S (I)	540.00	600.00	1400.00	1550.00	1924-S	800.00	900.00	3800.00	4200.00
1917-P (II)	375.00	415.00	1250.00	1400.00	1925-P	350.00	390.00	1250.00	1400.00
1917-D (II)	800.00	900.00	2250.00	2500.00	1926-P	350.00	390.00	1250.00	1400.00
1917-S (II)	800.00	900.00	2250.00	2500.00	1926-D	350.00	390.00	4000.00	4500.00
1918-P	540.00	600.00	1500.00	1675.00	1926-S	875.00	975.00	4500.00	5000.00
1918-D	975.00	1075.00	4500.00	500.00	1927-P	350.00	390.00	1250.00	1400.00
1918/17-S	15,000.00	—	35,000.00	—	1927-D	600.00	670.00	1750.00	1950.00
1918-S	540.00	600.00	4500.00	5000.00	1927-S	3600.00	4000.00	8000.00	9000.00
1919-P	540.00	600.00	1500.00	1675.00	1928-P	350.00	390.00	1350.00	1500.00
1919-D	1800.00	2000.00	8000.00	9000.00	1928-D	400.00	445.00	2350.00	2600.00
1919-S	1650.00	1825.00	7000.00	7850.00	1928-S	375.00	415.00	1350.00	1500.00
1920-P	425.00	470.00	1400.00	1500.00	1929-P	350.00	390.00	1150.00	1275.00
1920-D	1075.00	1200.00	3300.00	3650.00	1929-D	375.00	415.00	2500.00	2775.00
1920-S	600.00	675.00	4750.00	5250.00	1929-S	350.00	390.00	1150.00	1275.00
1921-P	1300.00	1450.00	4500.00	5000.00	1930-P	350.00	390.00	1150.00	1275.00
1923-P	525.00	585.00	2250.00	2500.00	1930-S	350.00	390.00	1300.00	1450.00

From: the *COIN DEALER newsletter* MONTHLY SUMMARY JUNE—1985:

STANDING LIBERTY QUARTERS

	MS-65 BID	MS-65 ASK	FULL HEAD MS-65 BID	FULL HEAD MS-65 ASK		MS-65 BID	MS-65 ASK	FULL HEAD MS-65 BID	FULL HEAD MS-65 ASK
1916-P	4250.00	4700.00	7300.00	7900.00	1923-S	1150.00	1300.00	4000.00	4400.00
1917-P (I)	900.00	950.00	2100.00	2325.00	1924-P	910.00	960.00	2200.00	2400.00
1917-D (I)	900.00	950.00	2250.00	2450.00	1924-D	930.00	980.00	2900.00	3200.00
1917-S (I)	915.00	965.00	2250.00	2450.00	1924-S	980.00	1030.00	3600.00	4000.00
1917-P (II)	900.00	950.00	2100.00	2325.00	1925-P	900.00	950.00	2100.00	2325.00
1917-D (II)	950.00	1000.00	2500.00	2700.00	1926-P	900.00	950.00	2100.00	2325.00
1917-s (II)	965.00	1015.00	2500.00	2700.00	1926-D	900.00	950.00	3600.00	4000.00
1918-P	910.00	960.00	2100.00	2323.00	1926-S	965.00	1015.00	4600.00	5000.00
1918-D	965.00	1015.00	4200.00	4500.00	1927-P	900.00	950.00	2100.00	2325.00
1918/17-S	15,000.00	—	30,000.00	—	1927-D	930.00	980.00	2200.00	2400.00
1918-S	950.00	1000.00	4200.00	4500.00	1927-S	2400.00	2650.00	8500.00	9100.00
1919-P	930.00	980.00	2100.00	2325.00	1928-P	900.00	950.00	2100.00	2325.00
1919-D	1600.00	1775.00	7500.00	8300.00	1928-D	910.00	960.00	2500.00	2700.00
1919-S	1500.00	1650.00	7000.00	7500.00	1928-S	910.00	960.00	2200.00	2400.00
1920-P	910.00	960.00	2100.00	2325.00	1929-P	900.00	950.00	2100.00	2325.00
1920-D	1000.00	1075.00	3200.00	3500.00	1929-D	910.00	960.00	2500.00	2700.00
1920-S	940.00	990.00	4500.00	4900.00	1929-S	900.00	950.00	2200.00	2400.00
1921-P	1100.00	1225.00	3850.00	4200.00	1930-P	900.00	950.00	2100.00	2325.00
1923-P	910.00	960.00	2200.00	2400.00	1930-S	900.00	950.00	2100.00	2325.00

From: the *COIN DEALER newsletter* MONTHLY SUMMARY JUNE—1986:

STANDING LIBERTY QUARTERS

	MS-65		FULL HEAD MS-65				MS-65		FULL HEAD MS-65	
	BID	ASK	BID	ASK			BID	ASK	BID	ASK
1916-P	3,900.	4,200.	6,700.	7,300.		1923-S	1,350.	1,450.	4,000.	4,400.
1917-P (I)	1,150.	1,250.	2,250.	2,450.		1924-P	1,100.	1,200.	2,575.	2,800.
1917-D (I)	1,150.	1,250.	2,500.	2,725.		1924-D	1,100.	1,200.	2,900.	3,200.
1917-s (I)	1,165.	1,265.	2,625.	2,850.		1924-S	1,215.	1,315.	3,300.	3,600.
1917-p (II)	1,100.	1,200.	2,250.	2,450.		1925-P	1,075.	1,175.	2,250.	2,450.
1917-D (II)	1,185.	1,285.	2,775.	3,000.		1926-P	1,075.	1,175.	2,250.	2,450.
1917-S (II)	1,200.	1,300.	2,775.	3,000.		1926-D	1,075.	1,175.	3,900.	4,400.
1918-P	1,100.	1,200.	2,250.	2,450.		1926-S	1,200.	1,300.	4,600.	5,000.
1918-D	1,200.	1,300.	4,200.	4,500.		1927-P	1,075.	1,175.	2,250.	2,450.
1918/17-S	15,000.	—	30,000.	—		1927-D	1,100.	1,200.	2,575.	2,800.
1918-S	1,185.	1,285.	4,200.	4,500.		1927-S	2,400.	2,650.	8,500.	9,100.
1919-P	1,100.	1,200.	2,250.	2,450.		1928-P	1,075.	1,175.	2,250.	2,450.
1919-D	1,600.	1,775.	7,500.	8,300.		1928-D	1,090.	1,190.	2,775.	3,000.
1919-S	1,500.	1,650.	7,000.	7,500.		1928-S	1,090.	1,190.	2,525.	2,750.
1920-P	1,075.	1,175.	2,250.	2,450.		1929-P	1,075.	1,175.	2,250.	2,450.
1920-D	1,215.	1,315.	3,200.	3,500.		1929-D	1,095.	1,190.	2,775.	3,000.
1920-S	1,125.	1,225.	4,500.	4,900.		1929-S	1,075.	1,175.	2,575.	2,800.
1921-P	1,300.	1,400.	3,850.	4,200.		1930-P	1,075.	1,175.	2,250.	2,450.
1923-P	1,100.	1,200.	2,675.	2,800.		1930-S	1,075.	1,175.	2,250.	2,450.

From: the *COIN DEALER newsletter* MONTHLY SUMMARY JUNE—1989:

STANDING LIBERTY QUARTERS

	MS-65		FULL HEAD MS-65				MS-65		FULL HEAD MS-65	
	BID	ASK	BID	ASK			BID	ASK	BID	ASK
1916-P	15,000.	—	16,000.	—		1923-S	2,700.	2,950.	5,500.	6,000.
1917-P (I)	1,900.	—	2,100.	2,300.		1924-P	1,700.	1,850.	2,800.	3,100.
1917-D (I)	2,100.	—	2,300.	2,500.		1924-D	1,700.	1,850.	4,900.	5,300.
1917-S (I)	2,300.	—	2,650.	2,850.		1924-S	2,150.	2,350.	7,000.	7,600.
1917-P (II)	1,700.	1,850.	2,500.	2,750.		1925-P	1,700.	1,850.	2,500.	2,750.
1917-D (II)	2,300.	2,500.	6,250.	6,800.		1926-P	1,700.	1,850.	3,500.	3,800.
1917-S (II)	2,400.	2,600.	5,800.	6,300.		1926-D	2,400.	2,600.	7,500.	8,200.
1918-P	1,700.	1,850.	2,600.	2,850.		1926-S	4,000.	4,400.	13,000.	—
1918-D	2,600.	2,800.	5,100.	5,600.		1927-P	1,700.	1,850.	2,600.	2,850.
1918/17-S	51,000.	—	65,000.	—		1927-D	1,700.	1,850.	5,600.	6,100.
1918-S	2,900.	3,200.	6,200.	6,700.		1927-S	7,650.	8,300.	13,000.	—
1919-P	1,800.	1,950.	2,500.	2,750.		1928-P	1,825.	2,000.	3,200.	3,500.
1919-D	4,500.	4,900.	9,700.	—		1928-D	1,700.	1,850.	3,500.	3,800.
1919-S	5,500.	6,000.	10,500.	—		1928-S	1,700.	1,850.	2,500.	2,750.
1920-P	1,700.	1,850.	2,700.	2,950.		1929-P	1,725.	1,875.	2,500.	2,750.
1920-D	2,800.	3,100.	4,500.	4,900.		1929-D	1,750.	1,900.	5,000.	5,500.
1920-S	5,000.	5,500.	6,800.	7,300.		1929-S	1,700.	1,850.	2,500.	2,750.
1921-P	2,400.	2,600.	5,400.	5,900.		1930-P	1,700.	1,850.	2,500.	2,750.
1923-P	1,700.	1,850.	2,900.	3,100.		1930-S	1,700.	1,850.	2,500.	2,750.

From: the *COIN DEALER newsletter* MONTHLY SUMMARY JUNE—1990:

STANDING LIBERTY QUARTERS

	MS-65	FULL HEAD MS-65		MS-65	FULL HEAD MS-65
1916-P	15,250.	—	1923-S	2,800.	5250.
1917-P (I)	1,750.	—	1924-P	950.	2,100.
1917-D (I)	1,800.	—	1924-D	950.	8,100.
1917-S (I)	1,950.	—	1924-S	2,850.	5,575.
1917-P (II)	950.	1,425.	1925-P	950.	1,425.
1917-D (II)	2,500.	5,325.	1926-P	950.	2,500.
1917-S (II)	1,925.	3,900.	1926-D	950.	18,250.
1918-P	1,050.	2,100.	1926-S	4,400.	15,000.
1918-D	2,100.	5,325.	1927-P	950.	1,800.
1918/17-S	52,000.	65,000.	1927-D	950.	3,200.
1918-S	2,500.	12,750.	1927-S	12,000.	13,500.
1919-P	1,000.	1,750.	1928-P	950.	2,300.
1919-D	3,600.	25,500.	1928-D	950.	4,600.
1919-S	4,000.	25,500.	1928-S	950.	1,425.
1920-P	950.	2,250.	1929-P	1,100.	1,425.
1920-D	2,350.	9,500.	1929-D	950.	4,550.
1920-S	3,550.	14,250.	1929-S	950.	1,425.
1921-P	3,000.	4,800.	1930-P	950.	1,425.
1923-P	950.	2,600.	1930-S	950.	1,425.

From: the *COIN DEALER newsletter* MONTHLY SUMMARY JUNE—1993:

STANDING LIBERTY QUARTERS

	MS-65	FULL HEAD MS-65		MS-65	FULL HEAD MS-65
1916-P	10,500.	15,500.	1923-S	1,350.	2,550.
1917-P (I)	800.	850.	1924-P	350.	945.
1917-D (I)	855.	1,375.	1924-D	350.	4,750.
1917-S (I)	900.	1,700.	1924-S	1,550.	4,000.
1917-P (II)	350.	800.	1925-P	350.	725.
1917-D (II)	1,000.	2,900.	1926-P	350.	1,060.
1917-S (II)	800.	2,500.	1926-D	365.	9,000.
1918-P	350.	960.	1926-S	1,800.	9,600.
1918-D	1,100.	4,350.	1927-P	360.	875.
1918/17-S	40,000.	60,000.	1927-D	350.	2,700.
1918-S	1,050.	8,500.	1927-S	7,000.	15,500.
1919-P	360.	775.	1928-P	420.	975.
1919-D	1,900.	11,000.	1928-D	350.	3,350.
1919-S	2,500.	11,000.	1928-S	350.	650.
1920-P	350.	1,000.	1929-P	350.	650.
1920-D	1,450.	4,800.	1929-D	350.	3,300.
1920-S	1,700.	12,500.	1929-S	350.	650.
1921-P	1,400.	2,600.	1930-P	350.	650.
1923-P	350.	1,200.	1930-S	350.	650.

STANDING LIBERTY QUARTERS

	MS-65	FULL HEAD MS-65		MS-65	FULL HEAD MS-65
1916-P	14,000.	23,500.	1923-S	1,850.	3,950.
1917-P (I)	725.	950.	1924-P	450.	1,575.
1917-D (I)	950.	1,500.	1924-D	480.	6,250.
1917-S (I)	1,650.	2,250.	1924-S	1,800.	7,000.
1917-P (II)	525.	850.	1925-P	470.	850.
1917-D (II)	1,400.	4,250.	1926-P	450.	1,650.
1917-S (II)	950.	3,700.	1926-D	525.	30,500.
1918-P	600.	1,450.	1926-S	1,900.	25,000.
1918-D	1,350.	5,350.	1927-P	440.	875.
1918-S	1,400.	18,750.	1927-D	475.	3,250.
1918/17-S	85,000.	300,000.	1927-S	9,500.	105,000.
1919-P	575.	1,050.	1928-P	430.	1,400.
1919-D	2,250.	22,000.	1928-D	440.	8,000.
1919-S	3,000.	30,000.	1928-S	450.	800.
1920-P	490.	1,700.	1929-P	445.	750.
1920-D	1,750.	6,900.	1929-D	485.	7,900.
1920-S	2,250.	32,000.	1929-S	435.	775.
1921-P	1,650.	4,250.	1930-P	430.	700.
1923-P	505.	3,900.	1930-S	550.	1,000.

QUOTES WITHOUT COMMENT

Henry Chapman, a dealer in Philadelphia, was enjoying good sales of the new 1916 quarters for $1.00 each and the new Denver and San Francisco half dollar at the same price. The new quarter, with only 52,000 minted, was already scarce. Within two years, Mr. Chapman advanced his price for the uncirculated 1916 Standing Liberty Quarter to $1.25 each and was selling worn pieces for $.55 each.

The total mintage of the Standing Liberty Quarter is 12,305,200 for the Type I and 212,516,800 for Type II, making a total of 224,822,000 which is 48,482,004 less than the 1964 Philadelphia Kennedy Half at 273,304,004. This is one of the least amount of off-center, clipped planchets, off medals, in other words, the least amount of errors in any U.S. coin in the twentieth century.

Concerning the price and quantity evaluation. The author has repriced all of the coins of this series in relation to what their true scarcity is. They have been arranged in a comparison chart so that you, the collector, can see how some of the coins, even at today's tremendously increased prices, from 1951 would still make an excellent collectible item. Many coins are underpriced in this series as most people are not familiar with this series of coins. To date, there are one or two reference books on this series but I do not believe any of them have given you, the collector, a chart showing a comparison in price, quantity etc. Also, on each date throughout this book your author has put down the price and quantity for that date and mintmark.

Date: All MS65 Full Head	Price	Quantity	Price Rank	Quantity Rank
1918/7-S	300,000.	UNKNOWN	1	1
1927-S	105,000.	396,000	2	3
1920-S	32,000.	6,380,000	3	25
1926-D	30,500.	1,716,000	4	10
1919-S	30,000.	1,836,000	5	12
1926-S	25,000.	2,700,000	6	17
1916	23,500.	52,000	7	2
1919-D	22,000.	1,944,000	8	14
1918-S	18,750.	11,072,000	9	30
1928-D	8,000.	1,627,600	10	9
1929-D	7,900.	1,358,000	11	5
1924-S	7,000.	2,860,000	12	18
1920-D	6,900.	3,586,400	13	20
1924-D	6,250.	3,112,000	14	19
1918-D	5,350.	7,380,000	15	26
1921	4,250.	1,916,000	16	13
1917-D Ty.II	4,250.	6,224,400	17	23
1923-S	3,950.	1,360,000	18	6
1923	3,900.	9,716,000	19	29
1917-S Ty.II	3,700.	5,552,000	20	21
1927-D	3,250.	976,000	21	4
1917-S Ty.I	2,250.	1,952,000	22	15
1920	1,700.	27,860,000	23	38
1926	1,650.	11,316,000	24	32
1924	1,575.	10,920,000	25	28
1917-D Ty.I	1,500.	1,509,200	26	7
1918	1,450.	14,240,000	27	37
1928	1,400.	6,336,000	28	24
1919	1,050.	11,324,000	29	33
1930-S	1,000.	1,556,000	30	8
1917, Ty.I	950.	8,740,000	31	27
1917, Ty.II	850.	13,880,000	32	36
1927	775.	11,912,000	33	34
1925	750.	12,280,000	34	35
1928-S	700.	2,644,000	35	16
1929	650.	11,140,000	36	31
1929-S	650.	1,764,000	37	11
1930	625.	5,632,000	38	22

STANDING LIBERTY QUARTERS
PRICE GUIDE FOR FULL HEADS ONLY AS OF JUNE, 1976

These are for M. S.65+, 65/70; even some of these prices are too low for M.S. 70. These prices are for the ultimate in strikes but not to be confused with 3/4 heads, 50% heads or even 90% heads, full heads with all three twigs showing above the roll of hair around the lower portion of Miss Liberty's head; as well as full shield, full knee and all toes. On some outstanding strikes, especially the Philadelphia Mint you could expect some hair detail from Miss Liberty's front curl to the back of her head. Coins of this description are few and far between.

Coins that do not fit this description are priced elsewhere in this book; such as the1926-D which is the classic example. This coin in uncirculated condition is available from $150.00 to the $4,000.00 category, so is the 1928-D and 1929-D.

Full Head	Price	Quantity	Price Rank	Quantity Rank
1918/17-S	$50,000.00	Unknown	1	1
1927-S	3,500.00	396,000	2	3
1919-D	3,500.00	1,944,000	3	14
1916	2,500.00	52,000	4	2
1919-S	2,500.00	1,836,000	5	12
1926-S	1,250.00	2,700,000	6	17
1923-S	1,250.00	1,360,000	7	6
1929-D	1,250.00	1,358,000	8	5
1920-S	975.00	6,380,000	9	25
1924-D	950.00	3,112,000	10	19
1926-D	950.00	1,716,000	11	10
1928-D	850.00	1,627,600	12	9
1924-S	850.00	2,860,000	13	18
1921	800.00	1,916,000	14	13
1918-D	750.00	7,380,000	15	26
1918-S	750.00	11,072,000	16	30
1920-D	700.00	3,586,400	17	20
1928-S	650.00	2,644,000	18	16
1917-S I	600.00	1,952,000	19	15
1917-D II	600.00	6,224,400	20	23
1917-S II	600.00	5,552,000	21	21
1930-S	600.00	1,556,000	22	8
1917-D I	550.00	1,509,200	23	7
1927-D	550.00	976,400	24	4
1917 II	450.00	13,880,000	25	37
1918	450.00	12,240,000	26	35
1920	450.00	27,860,000	27	38
1923	450.00	9,716,000	28	29
1924	450.00	10,920,000	29	28
1925	450.00	12,280,000	30	36
1926	450.00	11,316,000	31	32
1927	400.00	11,912,000	32	34
1928	400.00	6,336,000	33	24
1929	400.00	11,140,000	34	31
1929-S	400.00	1,764,000	35	11
1930	400.00	5,632,000	36	22
1917 I	395.00	8,792,000	37	27
1919	350.00	11,324,000	38	33

BIBLIOGRAPHY

American Numismatic Association, Colorado Springs, Colorado

Bowers & Merena

"The Coin Dealer Newsletter"

Coins and Collectors, Bowers, 1971

"The Evening News', September 19,1972 Newburgh, New York

Garhammer, John, Ph.D.

A Guide Book of United States Coins, R.S. Yeoman

Neidigh, Darrel, Hockessin, DE

Numismatic Scrapbook, December 1938

Numismatic Scrapbook, November 1940

Numismatic Scrapbook, Edgar Levy, March, 1945

Numismatic Scrapbook, 1963 Complete Chart

Numismatic Scrapbook, 1974, Amos Press, Sidney, Ohio

The Numismatist, 1918

Physical Culture, 1920 Edition

Reed, Mort. *Encyclopedia of US. Coins*

Schemmer, Rich, Franklin Square, NY

The Smithsonian Institution, National Numismatic Collection, Washington, D.C.

Stacks, New York, NY

Standing Liberty Quarters, Keith N. Kelman & Michael Turoff

United States Pattern Experimental and Trial Pieces, J. Hewitt Judd

Western Publishing Co., Inc.